Galatians
Walking in
God's Grace

Bruce BICKEL
&
Stan JANTZ

HARVEST HOUSE PUBLISHERS

EUGENE, OREGON

Unless otherwise indicated, all Scripture quotations are taken from the *Holy Bible,* New Living Translation, copyright ©2005. Used by permission of Tyndale House Publishers, Inc., Wheaton, IL 60189 USA. All rights reserved.

Verses marked NIV are taken from the HOLY BIBLE, NEW INTERNATIONAL VERSION®. NIV®. Copyright © 1973, 1978, 1984 by the International Bible Society. Used by permission of Zondervan. All rights reserved.

Verses marked TLB are taken from *The Living Bible,* Copyright ©1971. Used by permission of Tyndale House Publishers, Inc., Wheaton, IL 60189 USA. All rights reserved.

Cover by Left Coast Design, Portland, Oregon

Cover photo © Steve Terrill, Portland, Oregon, www.terrillphoto.com

Bruce Bickel is published in association with the literary agency of Mark Sweeney & Associates, 28540 Altessa Way, Ste. 201, Bonita Springs, FL 34135

Stan Jantz is published in association with the literary agency of Mark Sweeney & Associates, 28540 Altessa Way, Ste. 201, Bonita Springs, FL 34135

CHRISTIANITY 101 is a registered trademark of Bruce Bickel and Stan Jantz. Harvest House Publishers, Inc., is the exclusive licensee of the federally registered trademark CHRISTIANITY 101.

GALATIANS: WALKING IN GOD'S GRACE
Copyright © 2008 by Bruce Bickel and Stan Jantz
Published by Harvest House Publishers
Eugene, Oregon 97402
www.harvesthousepublishers.com

Library of Congress Cataloging-in-Publication Data

Bickel, Bruce, 1952-
　Galatians : walking in God's grace / Bruce Bickel and Stan Jantz.
　　p. cm. -- (Christianity 101)
　ISBN-13: 978-0-7369-2293-7
　ISBN-10: 0-7369-2293-8
　1. Bible. N.T. Galatians--Criticism, interpretation, etc. I. Jantz, Stan, 1952- II. Title.
BS2685.52.B53 2008
227'.407--dc22

2007044248

All rights reserved. No part of this publication may be reproduced, stored in a retrieval system, or transmitted in any form or by any means—electronic, mechanical, digital, photocopy, recording, or any other—except for brief quotations in printed reviews, without the prior permission of the publisher.

Printed in the United States of America

08　09　10　11　12　13　14　15　16　/　BP-NI　/　10　9　8　7　6　5　4　3　2　1

Contents

A Note from the Authors.................. 5

1. The Message of Galatians 13

2. This Is the Gospel....................... 25
   Galatians 1:1-10

3. Called by God.......................... 35
   Galatians 1:11-24

4. Diversity and Unity 45
   Galatians 2:1-10

5. When Leaders Collide 55
   Galatians 2:11-21

6. Justified by Faith....................... 65
   Galatians 3:1-14

7. The Promise and the Law 75
   Galatians 3:15-29

8. From Slavery to Freedom................ 85
   Galatians 4:1-11

9. Paul Gets Personal 95
   Galatians 4:12-20

10. A Story for the Ages 105
    Galatians 4:21-31

11. It Is for Freedom That Christ Set Us Free 115
    Galatians 5:1-12

12. New Life in the Spirit 127
       Galatians 5:13-26

13. Living to Please the Spirit 137
       Galatians 6:1-18

    Dig Deeper 147

A Note from the Authors

*L*ife is one big evaluation. From the earliest time you can remember, people have been measuring you, grading you, choosing you (or not choosing you), accepting you, and rejecting you. It's a never-ending process. We are constantly being evaluated by our performance, whether it's in school, a job, a contest, or sometimes even in church.

Don't you wish sometimes that other people saw you for who you are rather than for what you do? Well, there is at least one person who sees you for who you are, and He's the one who really counts. We're talking about God, of course. People may look on the outside, but God looks at the heart.

Knowing that should be an encouragement to you, but it could also be a little unsettling. If you're like we are, you are so used to performing that you have probably done your share of performing for God. If that's the case, then you've come to the right book—the book of Galatians. Here is a book—a letter actually—that will open your mind and your heart to a very important and life-changing truth: God loves you and accepts you for the person you are, not for the things you do.

As you make your way through this study on Galatians, you are going to come to appreciate what God has done for you in Christ, and how God has enabled you to live for Him in the power of the Holy Spirit.

Just a Little Help

The last thing the world needs is another commentary on Galatians. That's why we've taken a different approach in this guide to one of the great books of the Bible. Let's face it—there are lots of scholarly books that will give you the technical and theological concepts behind Galatians (we know, we've read some of them). If you want to dig into the original language of Paul's letter, you can find a commentary that will bring out the meanings of the Greek words. But if you simply want a book to help you understand Galatians and what it means to you personally, then this is the book you need to read.

Our approach to Bible study is very simple. We won't get in the way of your own personal study, but we will guide and encourage you along the way. In the first chapter, you will get some of the background of Galatians. We will give you the key themes and verses of the letter. In the other 12 chapters, we will walk through Galatians with you, helping you to understand what it means—and what it means to you. We are confident that Galatians will change the way you live as you discover the amazing things God has done for you.

Christianity 101™ Bible Studies

This Bible study on Galatians is part of a series called Christianity 101 Bible Studies. We've designed this series to combine the biblical content of a commentary with the life applications of a Bible study. By reading this book and answering the questions, you will learn the basics of what you need to know so you will get more meaning from the Bible. Not only that, but you will be able to apply what the Bible says to your everyday Christian life.

And just in case you want even more help in your study of God's Word, we have listed some books that were helpful to us in our study of Galatians. You'll find these at the end of the book in a section called "Dig Deeper." In addition, we have put together online resources especially for users of the Christianity 101™ Bible Studies series. All you have to do is click on www.conversantlife.com/101 (see page 151 for details).

This Book Is for You

Maybe this is your first time using a resource for studying the Bible, or maybe you are an experienced Bible student. Either way, we think this book is for you if...

- Reading the Bible is sometimes a little confusing for you. You get the overall picture, but you want additional information and insights to help you better understand how the Bible fits into your life and the world around you.

- You enjoy reading the Bible, but you don't think you're getting enough out of it. Sometimes it seems like the Bible isn't much more than a history book or a collection of wise sayings. You want the Bible to come alive and change the way you live.

- You and a few friends want to study a book of the Bible together, and you figure Galatians is a good place to start. You don't want a Bible study that will force you all to come to the same conclusions. You want a book that will give everyone room to think for themselves.

A Few Suggestions Before You Begin

We're ready to give you a little help, but we want to stay in the background. We aren't your teachers as much as we are your guides, explaining a few things and showing you some points of interest along the way. The Holy Spirit is your teacher, and He's the best there is. He will show you everything you need to know about Galatians and how it applies to your Christian life.

It was to us God revealed these things by his Spirit. For his Spirit searches out everything and shows us God's deep secrets (1 Corinthians 2:10).

We are convinced that as you study the letter of Galatians, God will speak directly to you through His Word and through the inner voice of the Holy Spirit. Our prayer is that your study of Galatians will change your life as you understand what God has done for you through Christ.

If You Are Studying Galatians on Your Own

- Have your Bible open to Galatians.
- Pray and ask God to help you understand His Word.
- Before you begin, read Galatians all the way through to get an overview. Don't worry about getting all the meaning and application.
- As you work through each chapter in this guide, try to understand the themes and arguments of Galatians,

as well as the book's context in the larger scope of the Bible.

- Write out your answers to the questions at the end of each chapter. Writing your thoughts down will reinforce what you are learning.

- Thank God for the wonderful riches of His Word and all that He has given you in Christ Jesus.

If You Are Studying Galatians in a Group

- Come prepared by doing everything suggested for individual study.

- Be a willing participant in the discussions, but don't dominate the conversation.

- Encourage and affirm the other people in your group as they talk.

- Be open and honest in your answers. If you don't understand something, admit it! Someone else may have the answer you're looking for.

- Sharing what a particular passage means to you is okay, but first you should try to discover what it means to everyone. Remember, biblical truths aren't different for different people.

- If someone shares something confidential, keep it in the group. At the same time, avoid turning your group Bible study into a gossip session.

- Pray for the other members of your group on a regular basis. Here's how Paul prayed for a group of Christians in his day:

We have not stopped praying for you ever since we first heard about you. We ask God to give you complete knowledge of his will and to give you spiritual wisdom and understanding. Then the way you live will always honor and please the Lord, and your lives will produce every kind of good fruit. All the while, you will grow as you learn to know God better and better (Colossians 1:9-10).

That's our prayer for you as well, so let's get started!

> Grace is the free, undeserved goodness and favor of God to mankind.
>
> —*Matthew Henry*

A Letter for Every Christian

Galatians has been called many things. Because it stands firmly on the bedrock of salvation through God's grace by faith alone in Christ alone, it has been called the catalyst for the Reformation. (Martin Luther was so fond of Galatians that he referred to it as his "wife.") Because it defends the true freedom of the Christian, it has been called the "Magna Carta" of Christianity. And because it explains how to live in the power of the Holy Spirit, many people consider it a key to living a spiritually fruitful life.

Whatever you call it, Paul's letter to the Galatians is a letter every Christian should read and study over and over again, for nowhere will you find a clearer statement for the true nature of the gospel of Jesus Christ. Even though it was written nearly two thousand years ago to people living in a different culture than yours, the issues Paul deals with in Galatians are as real and relevant in the twenty-first century as they were in the first. So get ready for a timeless treasure trove of truth that will help you walk in God's grace by understanding what Christ has done for you.

Chapter 1

The Message of Galatians

What's Ahead

- Grace and Freedom in Christ
- A Little Bit About Paul
- Done, Not Do

race is a wonderful word. When applied to humans, it means elegance or beauty of form. It can also imply consideration or goodwill. But when applied to God, the word *grace* takes on much more importance. First, God's grace tells us that He showed us favor when He didn't have to. Second, grace describes the process whereby God gave Himself to us in the person of Christ in order to forgive us and set us free from sin. The thing about God's grace is that, by definition, it is "unmerited favor." If you try to merit it—earn it—you can't get it. And without grace, there's no way to have freedom from sin.

Grace and Freedom in Christ

This is the message Paul brought to the Galatians—the liberating message of God's love and grace. In AD 47 Paul embarked on a journey (the first of four missionary journeys he would make in his lifetime) throughout the southern part of the Roman province known as Galatia. He delivered this message of God's grace and freedom in Christ as he stopped in such cities as Derbe, Lystra, Iconium, and Antioch of Pisidia (see Acts 13–14). Jews and Gentiles alike embraced Paul and received his Good News message, and several churches were planted in the region.

However, within just a few months, Paul's gospel of grace and freedom was challenged by a "different" gospel of law and works. This competing message was delivered by "false teachers" known as *Judaizers*, who taught that faith in Christ was not enough to gain God's approval. According to the Judaizers, you also needed to do certain things and perform certain rituals in order to be saved.

Who Were the Judaizers?

The *Judaizers* were Jewish Christians who insisted that salvation by faith alone was not enough. These teachers, who most likely came to Galatia from Jerusalem, said that certain traditions and rituals from Judaism (such as circumcision) were necessary for salvation and living the Christian life. In order to undermine Paul's message of salvation by faith alone, the Judaizers conducted a smear campaign against Paul, claiming he wasn't a true apostle and therefore lacked the authority necessary to validate his message.

When Paul got wind that the Judaizers were deliberately and systematically undermining his authority and discrediting his message, he responded with a stirring epistle, or letter, which he sent to the Galatians from his home base in Antioch of Syria. In his letter, Paul offered the Galatians a clear, concise, and convincing case for the true nature of the gospel of Christ—lived in the Spirit—and its superiority to the false gospel of the law—lived in the flesh.

In a series of three major arguments, Paul shows that the Spirit and flesh are in opposition. Consequently, he asks the Galatians to reject the false gospel advanced by the Judaizers—that we are justified by what we do—and to once again embrace the true gospel taught by Paul and the Scriptures—that we are justified *by faith alone*.

Galatians at a Glance

Author:	Paul the apostle
Date written:	AD 49
Written to:	The churches in southern Galatia established by Paul during his first missionary journey, and Christians everywhere
Type of Book:	An epistle, or letter
Setting:	Paul wrote Galatians while staying in Antioch of Syria
Purpose:	Paul counters the false gospel of works with the true gospel of grace
Major themes:	We are saved by God's grace; we receive God's gift of salvation in Christ by faith alone; we are no longer slaves to the law and to sin, but are free in Christ; we are called to live in the power of the Holy Spirit
Key verses:	Christ died for our sins (1:4); Christ lives in us (2:20); we are one in Christ (3:28); we are free in Christ (5:1)

A Little Bit About Paul

Before we get into our study of Galatians, let's take a quick tour of the life of Paul. Next to Jesus, there is no one more important to Christianity than the apostle Paul. Not only did Paul carry the gospel—or *Good News*—of Jesus Christ to the far reaches of the Roman Empire in the first century, but he also established the foundation of the Christian belief system through his letters to churches and individuals. Galatians is one of nine letters Paul wrote to the young churches in Asia Minor (present-day Turkey), Greece, and Italy. Paul also wrote four letters to individuals. Nearly 2000 years after he wrote his letters, churches and individuals around the world still read and study them in great detail.

His Early Life

Paul (his Roman name) was born Saul (his Jewish name) in Tarsus, an important commercial city and the capital of a Roman province. Tarsus was known for the production of *cilicium,* a cloth made of goat's hair that was commonly used to make sails, awnings, and tents. Paul learned the trade of tent making and later used it to support himself when he became a missionary. Because Paul was a Roman citizen by birth, he was able to travel freely throughout the Empire.

Sometime between the ages of 13 and 20, Paul moved to Jerusalem, where be began training to be a rabbi under the master teacher Gamaliel, whose grandfather founded the Pharisaic school. Because of his extensive rabbinical training, Paul probably knew more about Judaism than the Judaizers.

Saul the Persecutor

By his own account, Saul became "very zealous to honor God in everything" he did (Acts 22:3). That included persecuting the "followers of the Way, hounding some to death, arresting both men and women and throwing them in prison" (Acts 22:4). The most famous example of Saul's involvement in the killing of Christians occurred when Stephen, one of the leaders of the early church, became the church's first martyr.

ᴡhat Is a Martyr?

A martyr is someone who is put to death for professing their faith. *Martyr* comes from the Greek word for *witness*. And don't think for a minute that martyrdom is unique to the first century. According to the Voice of the Martyrs, an estimated 165,000 people were martyred in various parts of the world in the year 2000.

Saul stood by as Stephen was stoned to death (Acts 8:1). Following Stephen's martyrdom, Saul became the church's greatest enemy. He was a man possessed, "uttering threats with every breath." He was determined to "kill the Lord's followers" (Acts 9:1). Then something happened that dramatically changed Saul and the church forever.

From Saul to Paul

Acts 9 tells the incredible story of Saul's conversion from chief persecutor of the church to its main missionary. What a lesson for those of us who think there are some people who are "beyond saving." There is nobody outside the reach of God's amazing grace. There is not a single person, no matter how bad or how stubborn, who Jesus does not love. We would have given up on Paul. Worse, we would have prayed for his destruction! Not Jesus. He spoke to Paul while he was on his way to Damascus to arrest more Christians. Saul was knocked to the ground by a "light from heaven," and a voice called out, "Saul, Saul! Why are you persecuting me?"

When Saul asked who it was, Jesus replied, "I am Jesus, the one you are persecuting" (Acts 9:5). From that point forward Saul was spiritually transformed, and he became the Lord's "chosen instrument" to take the gospel of Jesus "to the Gentiles and to kings, as well as to the people of Israel" (Acts 9:15). As you can only imagine, Saul's conversion shocked the very Christians he had been persecuting. As we will see in our study, Paul had to "lay low" for a while, but he used that time to learn more about his Savior and Lord.

Paul the Missionary

As we look back on the life of Paul, we can see why God chose to convert him at this particular time. God needed someone to take the Good News of Christ to the ends of the earth. Up to this point, the believers had been staying close to their home base in Jerusalem. Then Stephen was killed, and the persecution of all believers in Jerusalem intensified, forcing the Christians to flee to Judea and Samaria (Acts 8:1).

This was what Jesus wanted all along: for His followers to go into all the world. Just before He left the earth and ascended into heaven, He gave a very specific command, sometimes called "The Great Commission":

> *You will receive power when the Holy Spirit comes upon you. And you will be my witness, telling people about me everywhere—in Jerusalem, throughout Judea, in Samaria, and to the ends of the earth* (Acts 1:8).

So you see, God even used the persecution by Saul and others to accomplish His purpose, scattering the believers so they could reach the world with the true gospel message:

Salvation is by God's grace, through faith alone, in Christ alone. There's nothing we can do to establish a right relationship with God except to believe in His Son and receive Him as our Savior and Lord.

Done, Not Do

As human beings, it's in our nature to do, to perform, to act. We are competitive. We want to win. But that's not the way it works in our relationship with God. Because God is utterly holy and perfect, His standard is perfection. And despite our best efforts—and because of our sin—we just can't measure up. The only chance we have is to accept God's grace by faith alone by trusting in God's plan to save us through Jesus Christ. The Christian life is about acceptance, not performance.

It's only fitting that Galatians is the first letter Paul wrote, because it contains this Good News message—for the Galatians and for us. The arguments Paul offers for why this message is true give us assurance. And the principles Paul lays out for how to live the Christian life give us confidence. We may scratch our heads and wonder why the Galatian Christians first accepted this message and then turned to another set of arguments and principles. But before we get too critical of them, we need to examine our own lives and see if we are enticed in any way by Christianity that is performance-based.

As you embark on this study, perhaps it would be a great idea to write out this phrase on a 3x5 card and tape it to your bathroom mirror as a reminder of what your life in Christ is all about:

DONE, NOT DO

These three little words contain the core themes of Galatians:

- Everything you need to get into a right relationship with God has been *done* through Christ;
- There's nothing you can *do* to earn God's favor except to receive Jesus by faith; and
- The only way to live the Christian life is to let the Holy Spirit control you.

May the Lord bless you as you incorporate these eternal truths into your life.

◼ ◼ ◼

$\mathcal{S}$tudy the $\mathcal{W}$ord

1. Why did you decide to study Galatians? What impressions of this letter did you have before starting this study? What do you hope to gain from this study?

2. Reflect on these two characteristics of God's grace, along with the Scripture for each one:
   - God showed us favor when He didn't have to (Ephesians 2:8-9)
   - God gave Himself to us in order to forgive us and set us free from sin (Galatians 1:3-4).

   Why did God show favor to sinful humanity? Why must God forgive us before He can set us free from sin?

3. Are there people today who insist, like the Judaizers did in the first century, that faith alone is not enough for salvation? What kinds of things and rituals do they add to salvation by faith alone?

4. Underneath each of these major themes in Galatians, write one benefit for you as a child of God:

    • We are saved by God's grace.

    • We receive God's give of salvation by faith alone.

    • We are no longer slaves to the law and to sin, but are free in Christ.

    • We are called to live in the power of the Holy Spirit.

5. Read the account of Saul's conversion in Acts 9:1-18. Give at least three reasons why you think Jesus chose Saul to carry out His name to Gentiles and their kings and the people of Israel.

6. As best you can, explain how God can use something like persecution for His own purposes. Do you think God *allows* such evil, or does He actually *cause* it?

7. What is the Good News message of Galatians?

There are two things to do about the Gospel—
believe it and behave it.

—*Susanna Wesley*

A Question of Character

Have you ever had anyone question your character? It's a tough spot to be in. In fact, when someone else makes statements—especially behind your back—that dispute your integrity, it affects all kinds of stuff: your reputation, your trustworthiness, and your words. In other words, negative statements about you, right or wrong, affect your character.

If you've ever been in that position, you know how Paul must have felt when he received word from Galatia that the Judaizers were questioning his character. Of course, it wasn't like these people were going to the media and smearing Paul in public. They were much more clever than that. No, these self-righteous individuals were planting little seeds of doubts in the minds of the Galatians. Can you hear the questions? "Who is this guy, Paul, anyway? Who does he think he is? He's not a real apostle because he wasn't a member of the original Twelve. Yet he calls himself an apostle, so he must have appointed himself. Do you think you can really trust a guy like that? Can you believe the things he is telling you?"

As you read the opening verses of Paul's letter to the Galatians, put yourself in Paul's place. People you don't even know are questioning your character. Even more, they are questioning your words and insinuating that you can't be trusted to tell the truth.

Chapter 2

This Is the Gospel

Galatians 1:1-10

*W*hat's *A*head

- ▪ The Authority of Paul and the Gospel of Christ (1:1-5)
- ▪ Faithless Galatians and False Teachers (1:6-7)
- ▪ The Consequence of Changing the Gospel (1:8-10)

*Y*ou can tell from the first few verses of Galatians that Paul is irritated. No doubt he's irritated with the Judaizers for questioning his character. And he is probably irritated with the Galatians for listening to the accusations. Normally, Paul opened his letters by showering the recipients with praise. He called the Ephesians "the faithful in Christ Jesus," and he referred to the folks in Colosse as "the holy and faithful brothers in Christ." Not so here. Paul dispenses with the formalities and simply writes, "To the churches of Galatia."

Yet as much as he is troubled by the attacks on his character and the way the Galatians have turned their backs on him, there is something that bothers him even more. The Galatians have turned their backs on God by questioning the way God has saved them.

On his previous visits, Paul had clearly taught the Galatians the truth that salvation is by faith alone in Christ alone. Now they were listening to the Judaizers, who taught that faith in Jesus was not enough. They said that if you wanted to be truly saved, you had to be circumcised and keep all of the law of Moses. In effect, they were saying that Christ's atoning death on the cross was not enough. In order to be accepted by God as righteous, you also needed to do the right things.

If ever there was a time in his life when Paul is spitting mad, this is it. So as he starts his letter, Paul directly answers the Judaizers' attacks and false claims.

The Authority of Paul and the Gospel of Christ (1:1-5)

We know that the Judaizers are challenging Paul's apostolic authority, because this is the first thing Paul deals with. In fact, being the brilliant and God-inspired writer that he is, Paul immediately lays out the three main arguments he is going to use in his letter:

- Paul has apostolic authority.
- God the Father planned everything.
- Jesus Christ has rescued us from this evil world.

Let's take a brief look at each of these.

Paul Has Apostolic Authority (1:1)

The false teachers have been telling the Galatians that Paul isn't an apostle. Paul wants to make sure they know he is an apostle, "sent not from men nor by man." Paul's call to ministry is from "Jesus Christ and God the Father, who raised him from the dead."

*W*hat's an *A*postle?

During the first century of the church, an apostle was personally appointed by Jesus Christ. There were 12 original apostles plus Matthias, who replaced Judas (Acts 1:12-26). Paul was also recognized as an apostle, because he was chosen personally by Jesus (Acts 9:20-26). These 13 men were commissioned by Jesus and given authority to establish and build the visible and universal church, of which Jesus is the cornerstone (Ephesians 2:10).

God the Father Planned Everything (1:1,3,4)

It was Jesus, of course, who personally initiated Paul's conversion and called him to ministry on the road to Damascus (read the dramatic story in Acts 9). But it was God the Father who planned it in order to rescue Paul from sin. Do you know that it's no different for you? You aren't called to be an apostle, but the risen Christ has called you to be His twenty-first-century follower and disciple (the word *disciple* means "learner"). This call—sometimes referred to as the "gospel call"—is not some afterthought on God's part. He loves you so much that He long ago planned everything out for your ultimate salvation.

Jesus Christ Has Rescued Us from This Evil World (1:4)

For us to be rescued from this evil world, Jesus had to die for our sins. Without that sacrifice for all the sins of all people—Paul's sins, the Galatians' sins, your sins, and our sins—there would be no salvation. There would be no way for us to be rescued from the sin, shame, despair, cruelty, tragedy, and temptations of this world. Being rescued *from* this evil world by Jesus does not mean we are rescued *out of* the world. But it means we are no longer obligated to follow the ways of the world. We are no longer enslaved to sin.

$\mathcal{T}$his $\mathcal{I}$s the $\mathcal{G}$ospel

Galatians 1:4 contains one of the most concise statements of the true gospel in all of Scripture. John Stott writes that this verse describes "the great historical event in which God's grace was exhibited and from which His peace is derived, namely the death of Jesus Christ on the cross." Three key elements are here:

1. *Christ died for our sins*—we are unable to save ourselves.

2. *In order to rescue us from this evil world in which we live*—Christ was sent to rescue us, not to take us out of this present world, but to give us hope there is a new world coming.

3. *Just as God our Father planned*—Christ gave Himself willingly according to God's will.

Faithless Galatians and False Teachers (1:6-7)

The Galatians had been taught all of this. They had accepted it. And God had called them "to Himself through the loving mercy of Christ" (1:6). They had experienced His love and mercy firsthand. And yet here they were, just a short time after Paul first introduced them to the Good News (that's what the word *gospel* means), deserting God and following a "different way." Understandably, Paul is "shocked."

Faithless Galatians

Paul isn't personally offended by the Galatians' actions. They haven't turned their backs on *him*. Rather, they have deserted Christ by rejecting the gospel of grace represented by Christ and His death on the cross, replacing it with a gospel of works represented by Moses and the law. Paul will develop this concept in more detail as the letter unfolds, but for now Paul is declaring to the Galatians that they have embraced another gospel. This "gospel" is not just a different version of the truth—it's a totally different message that is best summarized by the Judaizers' own creed:

> *Unless you are circumcised, according to the custom taught by Moses, you cannot be saved* (Acts 15:1).

Why Legalism Is Wrong

Trying to get right with God through good works, or by following the law, is called *legalism*. When it comes to our relationship with God, legalism is wrong not because laws are wrong, but because legalism replaces Jesus Christ. The rule of law can be useful, but rules or regulations that change or distort the gospel are not. By the way, the opposite of legalism is liberty. As his letter to the Galatians continues, Paul is going to show that while the gospel of works is all about legalism, the gospel of grace is all about liberty.

False Teachers

We can't take responsibility away from the Galatians, but there's a reason why they had turned away. They were being fooled by false teachers (the Judaizers) who were twisting and changing "the truth concerning Christ." The language Paul uses to describe this is strong. These false teachers weren't just modifying the truth. They were completely swapping the truth for a lie. In effect they were quick-change artists, and the result was a church in turmoil.

Look around at churches today. They don't get into trouble because of outside opposition. No, it's those on the inside who cause problems, and it's almost always because they try to change the truth concerning Christ. It may be someone teaching a class or small group. It could be someone opposing the pastor. Or it could be the pastor, preaching a "different way that pretends to be the Good News, but is not the Good News at all."

How do you know if this is happening in your church? The only way to discern a lie is to know the truth. Know what God has said in His word. Know what the gospel is all about. A lot of things have changed since the first century when Paul wrote this letter. Society and culture have changed, Christian lifestyles have changed, and the application of God's word has changed. But the original gospel of Jesus Christ has not changed, and anyone who alters it needs to be held accountable.

The Consequence of Changing the Gospel (1:8-10)

In our politically correct culture, it's unfashionable to condemn anyone for wrongdoing, especially if it involves a wrong viewpoint. Rather than holding people who distort the truth accountable, we would rather let them off the hook by saying something like "Well, you're entitled to your opinion." Not the apostle Paul. He isn't about to let the Judaizers off the hook, and so he pronounces a curse on them, and not just any curse. This is the major league of curses—God's curse. And just to make sure the Galatians know he isn't singling out any one person or group, Paul includes himself and the angels in the mix. In effect Paul is saying, "Let God's curse fall on *anyone* who preaches a different gospel."

You may think Paul is overreacting (after all, a curse is a serious thing), but here's what you have to realize. When the gospel is changed, two things happen:

- The work of Christ on the cross to secure our salvation is negated, meaning that Christ died for nothing; and

- Since Christ is the only way to be saved, anyone who trusts in the false gospel is lost.

We know, this is a sensitive issue for a lot of people these days—even Christians. People wonder how God can be so narrow-minded as to give us only one option for salvation. It's more popular to believe that in the end, God will also accept beliefs and forms of truth in addition to the truth found in Christ. Well, that may seem nice to think about, but it's horribly wrong. There is no "in addition to" when it comes to the truth found in Christ.

There is no indication in Scripture that God will accept any means of salvation other than what is provided "by Jesus Christ and God the Father, who raised him from the dead" (1:1). Even Jesus made it clear that He is the only way, the only truth, and the only life (see John 14:6). Any other truth is false and anyone who preaches any other truth is to be cursed.

■ ■ ■

Study the Word

1. Describe a time when someone seriously questioned your character. What did you do about it? What was the eventual outcome?

2. Why did the Judaizers question Paul's authority? Why is it important for Paul to establish that he is an apostle sent by Jesus, not from men or by man?

3. Most likely you haven't heard the voice of Jesus calling out to you like Paul did, but do you believe that Jesus has personally called you to be His follower and disciple? If you really believe this, how should this change the way you live?

4. If we are followers and disciples of Christ and are therefore no longer obligated to follow the ways of the world, why do we still follow the world's ways?

5. What are the main points of the "different way" or "different gospel" of the legalists? What are some current-day belief systems that embrace these points? Why do you think people are drawn to such beliefs?

6. Why is it important to know the original gospel of Jesus Christ? How do you know that the gospel you believe is the true gospel? What would you say to someone who thinks the beliefs of the church today have been changed over the years?

7. Do you think Paul is overreacting by cursing the Judaizers? What's the harm in letting false teachers express their opinions?

If God has called you, do not spend time
looking over your shoulder to see
who is following you.

—*Corrie ten Boom*

God Has Given You a Life Mission

After laying his cards on the table—the Galatians have
been deceived by false teachers, causing them to follow a
perverted gospel of works—Paul begins to make his case
for the true gospel of grace. Beginning in this section, and
continuing through the end of Galatians 2, Paul lays out
the first two of three proofs for the true gospel: *Paul has
apostolic authority, and the gospel he preached to the Galatians was not from man but from God.*

To do this, he gives a synopsis of his own conversion
story, reminding his readers that he was an intense persecutor of the Christian church before God saved and called
him through a special revelation of Jesus Christ. Paul then
gives a chronology of the years after his conversion and
call, making it clear that he didn't have contact with the
Jerusalem church and its leaders for the first three years of
his Christian life. He wants to make sure his Galatian readers
know that his authority came directly from Jesus.

The dramatic story of Paul's conversion is not meant to
be a template for your own conversion experience. Most
Christians can't claim a special revelation from Christ as
Paul did. But like Paul, you have a unique and God-given
mission in life, and it's something God planned for you
long ago.

Chapter 3
Called by God

Galatians 1:11-24

What's Ahead

- From the Highest Authority (1:11-12)
- Paul's Conversion, Call, and Hidden Years (1:13-17)
- Paul Goes to Jerusalem (1:18-24)

Not long ago we were on a business trip to New York City. As we were walking to an appointment, we noticed street vendors selling all kinds of brand-name knockoffs. There were guys selling fake Rolex watches, guys selling fake Chanel perfume, and guys selling fake Louis Vuitton purses. Being the good husbands we are, we decided to buy our wives fake purses. To our eyes, they looked just like real Louis Vuitton purses, at a fraction of the cost. We couldn't go wrong!

The problem was when we got home. It didn't take our wives five seconds to spot the fakes, and they called us on it. We had bought into the lie, and they recognized it. The only good thing about it was that we all laughed about it, and no real harm was done (except to solidify our reputations as cheapskates).

Like the two of us buying fake purses on the streets of New York, the Galatians have bought a fake version of the true gospel, and Paul has called them on it. Only the consequences of their actions are a lot more serious than ours. Paul is very concerned about this, which is why he is now building a meticulous case to prove that the gospel of grace is the genuine article. In this section he argues that the gospel he preached to them was the true gospel straight from God through a "direct revelation from Jesus Christ" (1:12).

From the Highest Authority (1:11-12)

The Judaizers knew that the most effective way to undermine the message of grace and liberty was to undermine the authority of its greatest proponent—the apostle Paul. They did this by suggesting that Paul wasn't a true apostle, which implied he got his Good News message from a human source. Paul reminds the Galatians that he received the gospel message directly from Jesus, the highest authority possible. Paul makes it clear that "no one [else] taught me" (1:12). He received his apostolic authority independent of any other source, in particular the other apostles in Jerusalem.

No wonder Paul is so perplexed at the Galatians' actions. How could they so willingly reject Paul's authority, which came from Jesus Christ, and so easily accept the message from the Judaizers, who were mere men?

Paul's Conversion, Call, and Hidden Years (1:13-17)

What Paul does next is a great example for the rest of us to follow. When someone questions the things we are saying about Jesus, we need to do what Paul does here and tell our story, specifically how Jesus *converted* us from our former life and *called* us to Himself.

How Does Conversion Happen?

Conversion is a dynamic and supernatural process that theologian Wayne Grudem defines as "our willing response to the gospel call, in which we sincerely repent of sins and place our trust in Christ for salvation." Conversion involves *turning away* from sin (that's what it means to *repent*) and *turning toward* Christ (that's what it means to *trust*). We bring nothing to the table in the process of our conversion except for faith—but it's not a "blind" faith or a "leap in the dark." Faith includes both *believing* that God's plan to save us in Christ Jesus is true, and also *trusting* Christ to forgive us of sins and to make us right with God.

Paul's story is dramatic. He was a violent persecutor of Christians. Luke the physician, who wrote one of the four biographies of Jesus—known as the four Gospels—as well as the history of the early church in the book of Acts, writes that Paul was "uttering threats with every breath" (Acts 9:1). Saul (as Paul was known before his conversion) wasn't some rogue opponent of the early Christian church. He was a learned and respected Jewish student and teacher. In fact, he was even more zealous than the Judaizers who were now worming their way into the Galatians' confidence.

Conversion and Call

Then "something happened"—something so dramatic and earth-shattering that the only explanation is supernatural. Paul describes it in a simple sequence (1:15-16):

- God chose and called him even before he was born;
- God showed grace to him; and
- God revealed His Son to him.

If you have trusted Jesus Christ as your personal Savior and Lord, then you can be sure that you have experienced the same thing. Before you were born—even before the world was created—God chose you (Ephesians 1:4). As a sinner, you didn't deserve the free gift of salvation, but God gave you the gift of salvation anyway (that's the essence of grace). Maybe your conversion wasn't as dramatic as Paul's, but it was no less miraculous and no less significant. From a spiritual perspective, everything that happened to Paul happened to you. And just like Paul's story, the change in your life cannot be explained by logic or natural means. Your conversion was a supernatural event.

*Y*our *C*onversion and *C*all

Why did God save you? Have you ever thought about that? You can't say that God saved you because you're a good person, or because you were born into the right family, or because you've been going to church since you were a baby. None of that counts. "God saved you by his grace when you believed," Paul writes in his letter to the Ephesians. "And you can't take credit for this; it is a gift from God" (Ephesians 2:8).

God didn't save you because you deserved it, but He did save you for a reason. God saved Paul and then called him to take His Good News message about Christ to the Gentiles (Acts 9:15). Did you know that God saved and called you for a purpose? Paul tells us, "We are God's masterpiece. He has created us anew in Christ Jesus, so we can do the good things he planned for us long ago" (Ephesians 2:10). Whether you know it now or not, God has a purpose for you on earth, not just in heaven. Theologian G. Walter Hansen puts it this way: "Every Christian is unique and gifted by God for a special mission in life."

Hidden Years

You would think that once Paul's life was miraculously changed, he would have gone straight to Jerusalem, the center of Christian activity (where he could have been a big name on the Christian celebrity speaking circuit). But that wasn't what God had in mind. Rather than send Paul to Jerusalem, where he could have met the other apostles, God sent him to Arabia and Damascus for three years.

Walter Hansen calls these the "hidden years" because Paul doesn't tell us what he did during this time. But we can be pretty sure Paul wasn't wasting time. In all likelihood Paul went to Arabia in order to be alone with God in prayer and study. Through prayer he would have learned to know God intimately, and through study he would have learned about God in ways he never knew before.

What a contrast from our culture today! Rather than taking the time to prepare for the ministry God has for us, we want to jump right in and start, often before we are prepared. "But the mission is urgent," you might argue. Well, look at Paul's mission to the Gentiles. There's no question it was urgent, yet Paul took time to prepare himself before the Lord. And did his investment of time in these hidden years pay off? Absolutely. Students of Paul's theology believe that the effect of these three years was the Christian theology we see in his letter to the Romans—a theology that has guided the church for 2000 years.

Paul Goes to Jerusalem (1:18-24)

Paul eventually made it to Jerusalem to visit with Peter and James, the half-brother of Jesus, but he stayed only 15 days. His visit may have been cut short by opposition from influential Jews (Acts 9:29), or perhaps Paul was anxious to start preaching in Syria and Cilicia (1:21). Whatever the reason, Paul makes it clear to his Galatian readers that he spent three years alone with God and just 15 days in Jerusalem with the leaders of the church. His point is to further strengthen his authority and the authority of his message.

Paul even takes an oath—"I declare before God that what I am writing to you is not a lie"—to reinforce his point. Paul wants to absolutely contradict the false reports from the false teachers that he has received his gospel and his authority to preach from the apostles in Jerusalem.

Another strong confirmation of Paul's authority is the way his message was received among the churches in Judea. The Jewish Christians in this region, who didn't know Paul personally, gave glory to God because Paul was now preaching the gospel of grace and faith, the "very faith he tried to destroy."

■ ■ ■

$\mathcal{S}$tudy the $\mathcal{W}$ord

1. What would you say to someone who claimed to have received a message directly from Jesus Christ? What's the difference between Paul's revelation and authority and someone else claiming to have the same revelation and authority? (Hint—see the definition of an apostle in chapter 2.)

2. What is the story of your conversion and call? Use a sheet of paper to write out your story.

3. In what ways has God continued to show grace to you in your life? How has Jesus continued to reveal Himself to you?

4. What are some of the "good things" God has planned for you to do? Have you identified your special mission? If not, what could you be doing to find out?

5. From the example of Paul, we know how important it is to prepare for ministry. What have you done to prepare for your special mission or ministry? What could you be doing in the future? (Keep in mind that all of Christ's disciples are ministers, not just those who are in "full-time Christian service.")

6. Who are some other people in Scripture who took time to prepare for their special mission? What were the benefits to these people and their ministries?

7. When the churches in Judea welcomed Paul's message and praised God because of him, it was a confirmation of Paul's authority. What are some other things that confirm the validity and authority of someone's message?

The best place to start building unity in
the church is to start working with a team
of diverse people who are united by their
common faith in Christ and their mission.

—G. Walter Hansen

The Message Is Always the Same

So far in his first of three major arguments to the Galatians to prove that his gospel is true, Paul has made it clear that he received his apostolic authority directly from Jesus, independent of the other apostles in Jerusalem. As Galatians 2 begins, he continues this argument, but with a different emphasis. Now he lets the Galatians know that even though his gospel is *independent* of the other apostles, it is the *same* as theirs.

Evidently the Judaizers are trying to create a division between Peter, a leader in the Jerusalem church, and Paul, who is preaching in other places from his base in Antioch. So God instructs Paul to return to Jerusalem in order to affirm that Peter's message and Paul's message are the same. This section is a great example for us. Even though God calls us to different ministries in different places, our Good News message is always the same: The only way to be saved is through faith alone in Christ alone.

Chapter 4

Diversity and Unity

Galatians 2:1-10

*W*hat's *A*head

- Paul Confronts the Gospel of Works (2:1-5)
- Paul Puts the Judaizers in Their Place (2:6-10)

*A*s Galatians 2 opens, Paul writes that he went back to Jerusalem "fourteen years later." Scholars agree that he means 14 years after his conversion, not 14 years after his last visit to Jerusalem. What scholars don't agree on is the reason for the visit. One view has Paul, along with his two traveling companions, Barnabas and Titus, going there for the Jerusalem council (Acts 15). A second view has Paul traveling to Jerusalem with his buddies to deliver food in anticipation of a famine coming to the entire Roman world (Acts 11:27-30).

We like the second view for one simple reason. Paul writes that he went to Jerusalem because "God revealed to me that I should go." This seems to coincide with the prophecy given by the Holy Spirit and delivered by Agabus concerning the famine (Acts 11:28). Either way, the effect is the same: Paul travels to Jerusalem, where the church leaders accept him and his companions. More importantly, Paul's gospel message is accepted as well.

*H*eart and *H*ead *T*ogether

Paul says he was led by a "revelation" from God to go to Jeru-salem (2:2), but he doesn't say how the revelation came. It could have been a special revelation related to this visit, or it could have been a result of the way he was living his life, always sensitive to the leading of the Holy Spirit. However the revelation came, Paul obeyed, but not without using his head. He "felt" that God wanted him to go to Jerusalem, but he also "knew" how to pre-pare for the visit, and what to do once he got there.

So it should be with you. As you grow as a Christian, doing those good things God planned for you long ago, your life should be a wonderful blend of responding to God's promptings in your *heart* by using your *head* to carry out your assignments. Don't move forward on feelings alone. Like Paul, you should also draw upon your experience as a disciple of Christ, your knowledge of God's Word, and the advice of other mature Christians, to do God's will.

Paul Confronts the Gospel of Works (2:1-5)

Jesus once told His followers, "Be as shrewd as snakes and as harmless as doves" (Matthew 10:16). Wherever he went, Paul embodied this advice. Once he received his assign-ment from God, his actions were always a balance between wisdom ("shrewd as snakes") and discretion ("harmless as doves"). Take this trip to Jerusalem. He responds to God's call upon his heart and goes to Jerusalem, but not before arranging for Barnabas, his co-laborer and chief encour-ager, to help him transport the gifts of the believers in Antioch (Acts 11:30).

Before he begins his trip, however, Paul exhibits some "shrewd as snakes" wisdom. He decides to pick up Titus, a Gentile believer who also lives in Antioch. As we will find out, Paul doesn't ask Titus to join the team because he needs someone to carry his luggage. Paul is bringing Titus along as a kind of "test case" for the Jerusalem leaders. No doubt the Judaizers, who also used Jerusalem as their home base, have been pressuring the apostles to make circumcision a requirement for salvation. As a Gentile, of course, Titus was uncircumcised. So Paul, the shrewd rascal that he is, wants to find out how his fellow apostles in Jerusalem will respond.

*W*hat's the *B*ig *D*eal with *C*ircumcision?

If there were ever a "work of the law" that the legalists found sacred, it was circumcision. But why? What's the big deal? For one thing, circumcision was initiated by God as a sign of the covenant He made with Abraham (Genesis 17:10-14). Given before Abraham had any children with Sarah, circumcision symbolized Abraham's total dependence on God for the descendants God promised. Over time circumcision became an end in itself and a source of pride rather than a symbol of God's provision. Beyond that, since circumcision is essentially the "mark" of God's people under the law, then that mark is no longer necessary, since Christ fulfilled the law and God's covenant promise. He is the "mark" on our hearts.

Paul and His Merry Men (2:1-3)

Here comes Paul with his little missionary band—two Jews and a Gentile—basically confronting the issue of works vs. grace head-on. Can't you just see this bulldog and his friends marching into a meeting with the leaders of the church? Can't you just hear him saying, "Let's put our cards on the tables, boys. It's time to fish or cut bait!" That's the "shrewd as snakes" Paul.

The "harmless as doves" Paul confronts the Jerusalem church leaders in private. Here he demonstrates discretion and consideration for his fellow apostles, even though he isn't looking for their approval (remember, he already has God's approval). Rather, he wants to make sure their message is consistent with his. This is important to Paul. He needs the recognition—not the approval—of the mother church in order to continue his ministry to the Gentiles. If the leaders disagree, Paul is afraid that he has been running his "race in vain" (2:2 NIV).

$\mathcal{P}$aul the $\mathcal{A}$thlete

Paul must have been a sports enthusiast, because he often uses analogies from athletics in his letters to make a point. In his letter to the Philippian church, he says that he wants to "reach the end of the race and receive the heavenly prize for which God, through Christ Jesus, is calling us" (Philippians 3:14). In his letter to his disciple Timothy (the last letter Paul would write), he says, "I have fought the good fight, I have finished the race" (2 Timothy 4:7). And here in Galatians, he confides that he doesn't want to run his race in vain.

Snakes in the Parlor (2:4-5)

Although Paul tries to keep the meeting with the Jerusalem apostles private, the Judaizers—Paul refers to them as "so-called Christians" and "false teachers"—crash the party. Their purpose is clear: They want to enslave the Christians by requiring them to follow Jewish regulations. Larry Richards writes colorfully that what you have here is the "Freedom Party" (Paul, Barnabas, Titus) squaring off against the "Slavery Party" (the Judaizers). And in the middle of the confrontation are the "pillars of the church"

(James, Peter, and John), who need to cast their votes. Which party will they choose?

Thankfully, the leaders agree with Paul. Nothing needs to be added to faith, especially not circumcision (the huge sigh of relief you are hearing is from Titus).

Paul Puts the Judaizers in Their Place (2:6-10)

It isn't even a contest. The Judaizers and their "salvation by works" gospel don't stand a chance against Paul and his "salvation by grace" gospel. And it has nothing to do with James, Peter, and John wisely recognizing that Paul has been divinely commissioned to preach the gospel to the Gentiles. Yes, they did that, but as Paul writes, "The leaders of the church had nothing to add to what I was preaching" (2:6).

Paul isn't disrespecting them. To the contrary, he has a lot of respect for God's appointed leaders, as you should. Paul recognizes that Peter has also been appointed by God, only his calling is to preach to the Jews. When Paul says that the leaders have nothing to add to his message, he means that they find Paul's gospel completely true. There is nothing they can add to make it any better or more true.

Diversity and Unity

If this recognition of Paul's message is a huge setback for the Judaizers, then the leaders' acceptance of Paul and his boys as "their co-workers" is a kick in their collective stomach. Talk about disrespecting! The Judaizers had hoped to discredit Paul and his gospel in front of the apostolic leaders in Jerusalem. That was never going to happen. In God's perfect plan, Paul's Gentile mission is of equal importance to Peter's Jewish mission, and God's true apostles recognize this without question.

Whereas in chapter 1 of Galatians, Paul stresses his independence from the other apostles, in this chapter he shows there is unity between them. What a marvelous example for us! In the body of Christ, there is room for *diversity* of spiritual gifts, approaches, and audiences. But when it comes to the truth of the gospel and the person of Jesus, there should always be *unity.*

Help the Poor

Before we move on to the second half of Galatians 2, there is one more thing we need to consider. Notice in 2:10 how Paul talks about the only suggestion the Jerusalem leaders make: They want him to remember to help the poor. Paul endorses this admonition, showing that he is a person of compassion. No doubt he recognizes that when we help the poor, we are acting out of obedience to Christ to demonstrate the gospel of grace in tangible ways.

■ ■ ■

$\mathcal{S}$tudy the $\mathcal{W}$ord

1. Give an example of how you can use your heart and head together in the following hypothetical situations:

   • determining the nature of your special mission

   • deciding whether or not to enter a particular vocation

- discovering and using your spiritual gift (or gifts)

2. It's difficult for us to understand why circumcision was such a big deal to the Jews and the Judaizers. Can you think of a ritual some churches have established as a "works" requirement for salvation, spiritual growth, or both?

3. Paul understood that, while he didn't need the approval of the church leaders, he needed their recognition. Why was this important to Paul? Think about your own ministry for a moment. Can you follow Paul and seek out the recognition but not the approval of your church or spiritual leaders? Why or why not?

4. Name some qualities or characteristics of athletics that make it such an ideal analogy for the Christian life. What are some ways you could use athletics to talk to an unbeliever about Jesus?

5. Where do false teachers come from? Why are they so intent on undermining the true gospel of Jesus? What is their motivation? What do they hope to gain?

6. Why is a "salvation by works" gospel inferior to a "salvation by grace" gospel? Give at least three reasons.

7. Give three reasons why diversity is necessary in the body of Christ. Give three reasons why unity is essential.

Christ is the sole meaning of life for Paul: every moment is passed in conscious dependence on Christ, to whom he looks for everything. This is Christian faith, and it is intensely personal.

—R. Alan Cole

Confronting for the Right Reason

It's one thing to stand in opposition to someone who opposes you, but what do you do when one of your friends does something you know to be wrong? Do you let it go and hope they will come to see the "error of their ways," or do you confront your friend and risk the friendship? Paul now finds himself in such a predicament with one of his friends and co-workers, who just happens to be a church leader. Talk about a tough situation!

The way Paul deals with his friend, Peter, is a fascinating study of confrontation. We're not necessarily suggesting that you use Paul's methods (as you will see, he calls Peter out publicly), but you need to imitate his courage. Confrontation for the right reason is never easy, but it is necessary and beneficial.

*C*hapter 5

When Leaders Collide

Galatians 2:11-21

*W*hat's *A*head

- Paul Confronts Peter (2:11-13)
- The Difference Between Peter and Paul (2:14-16)
- Crucified with Christ (2:17-21)

*A*s Paul continues his letter to the Galatians, he comes to the end of his personal story. As we stated previously, the purpose of his mini-autobiography, which begins in 1:11, is to show that his message is from God, not men. So far Paul has made two points in this phase of his argument. One, he was given his authority by God independent of the other apostles. Two, his authority and message were recognized by the other apostles.

Now he is about to show that his authority gives him the right to challenge the other apostles. By doing this, Paul shows we should confront not only those who oppose the gospel (such as the Judaizers), but also those who embrace the true gospel but act hypocritically (such as Peter). The bottom line is that the truth of the Good News message of the gospel must be followed, no matter what.

Paul Confronts Peter (2:11-13)

Paul's letter isn't specific as to how this next incident happened, but it's safe to assume that soon after Paul, Barnabas, and Titus left Jerusalem and returned to Antioch, Peter came for a visit. When Peter arrived, he saw Gentile and Jewish Christians eating together, something that was still a rarity in the early church. You see, dietary laws were an important part of Jewish tradition because they served to give Jews a sacred identity by separating them from Gentiles. But that was under the law.

As we're going to see, the law represents human effort, which does nothing to make us right before God. Only by turning from our sins to God and accepting His forgiveness in the name of Jesus can we be saved—Jews and Gentiles alike. God even showed Peter in a vision that the dietary laws were no longer a barrier between Jews and Gentiles because God isn't partial to any one group (Acts 10:9-15, 28). Evidently Peter ate with the Gentile believers when he first arrived in Antioch, showing the unity that all believers have in Christ.

The Significance of Sharing a Meal

In Galatians 3:28 Paul writes what was to become the Magna Carta of the young Christian church: "There is no longer Jew or Gentile, slave or free, male or female. For you are all Christians—you are one in Christ Jesus." Nothing illustrated this powerful statement for freedom and liberty in Christ more than Jews and Gentiles sharing a meal together. In the first century sitting down to eat with friends showed great respect and unity. Unfortunately, this unity was shattered by Peter's behavior.

Peter Bends to Pressure

Just as things are going well in Antioch, those meddling Judaizers show up and spoil the party. (Paul refers to them as "Jewish friends of James," but they were probably not sent by James.) These are likely the same guys who were kicked in the gut by Paul in Jerusalem. Their circumcision tactic didn't work, so they decide to play a new hand—and it works with at least one influential individual. Afraid of what these "legalists" would say, Peter decides he can no longer share a meal with the Gentile believers.

Why did Peter cave in to the Judaizers? Well, we know from past history that Peter has trouble standing up to peer pressure (remember his three denials?). Maybe Peter was afraid he would offend the Jewish community in Jerusalem. Whatever the motivation, Peter's action is wrong for three reasons:

- By refusing to share a meal, Peter turns the table of unity into a table of separation;
- By his action, Peter is teaching that there are two bodies of Christ; and
- Peter's action of hypocrisy (believing one thing and doing another) causes others—including Barnabas—to act hypocritically.

Paul Gets Tough

Paul very quickly sees that not only has Peter done the wrong thing, but his action has also harmed the gospel message. So Paul has to "oppose him to his face, for what he did was very wrong" (2:11). What a contrast between these two early church leaders:

- Paul fought for the freedom in Christ found in the gospel;
- Peter wilted under the pressure and threat of persecution.

The Difference Between Peter and Paul (2:14-16)

Because Paul sees Peter as betraying Christian liberty, he confronts Peter "in front of all the others" (2:14). As we said earlier, confronting someone in public isn't necessarily the best way to handle disputes between Christians. Jesus advised us to go to the offending party in private first, and then if there's no repentance, to bring the matter before the church (Matthew 18:15-17). It's possible that Paul did go to Peter privately at first, but with no result. Or Paul may have felt that Peter's very public wrong deserved a public response. Either way, Paul is very passionate in his reprimand because Peter's action isn't just hypocritical. Much worse, it is theologically wrong and very dangerous.

Why Peter Was Wrong

We know that Peter knew the true gospel. That wasn't the problem. The big problem was that Peter was living in contradiction to the truth. In effect, his actions were saying that faith plus adherence to Jewish law were necessary for acceptance by God. Peter compromised the gospel by trying to make Gentiles become Jews.

How about you? Is there anything you are doing that contradicts what you know to be true about the Good News message of the gospel? By your actions or your words, are you withdrawing from the "table of unity" that includes other believers who may have different backgrounds and traditions than you do? Are you adding anything to your relationship with God? Remember that as you live your Christian life, actions speak louder than words.

Why Paul Was Right

As we said earlier, Paul's strong statement for the unity of the body of Christ is found in Galatians 3:28. In Christ, there aren't any ethnic, social, or gender barriers. And there is nothing we can do to earn God's favor. Paul's tireless message is that we are made right with God—the theological term is *justified*—only by believing and receiving God's gracious gift of salvation through faith alone in Christ alone, not by obeying the law.

*J*ustification by *F*aith

The concept of justification by faith is the bedrock of Christian doctrine, and Paul is its most eloquent spokesman. Paul knew that in order to be saved, we have to admit that our good works—no matter how good—cannot make us right with God. Christ fulfilled the law in that He kept it perfectly, but as the revealed Word of God, He went beyond the law. When we try to keep the law after Christ has already made His sacrifice for our sins, we effectively deny His sufficient work. It means we go back in history to a period before Christ came. For Paul, this is unacceptable, for it denies the very reason why Christ came.

Crucified with Christ (2:17-21)

One of the arguments the Judaizers were using against the principle of justification by faith was this: If salvation is based on faith alone, and not by any works or good deeds, then what keeps us from sinning? To put it more bluntly, they believed justification by faith encourages sinful living.

Paul refutes this idea because it implies that Christ leads us to sin (2:17).

Despite this terrible implication, people today are still using this argument. They think that grace encourages sin, so they try to work their way to God. Of course, this reasoning can backfire. Like an employee trying to climb the corporate ladder, they operate on the principle that a superior performance will earn them a good job review from the Big Boss. The problem is, nobody is capable of a "superior performance," so people often get discouraged and go the other way, plunging into a life of sin.

Then there are those who don't think they're "good enough" for God. When people believe they have to "clean up their act" before they come to Christ, they usually don't take that necessary step of faith, because they never feel worthy.

But isn't that the point of faith? None of us is "good enough" on our own. All of us are sinners (Romans 3:23). Because of that sin, none of us willingly seeks God (Romans 3:11), and there's no amount of law-keeping that will give us right standing before God. That's why Paul writes, "When I tried to keep the law, it condemned me" (2:19a). Paul then makes a statement that sums up how it is possible for sinners to live the Christian life:

> So I died to the law—I stopped trying to meet all its requirements—so that I might live for God. My old self has been crucified with Christ. It is no longer I who live, but Christ lives in me (Galatians 2:19b–20a).

When Christ died, He died for us. He did what we could never do—live a perfect life—and then He took on Himself God's anger against sin. When we accept by faith what

Jesus did on our behalf, we admit that our good works can
never help us, and we invite Him to live His life in us. As
Paul says, we have been "crucified with Christ," and now
Christ lives in us. Larry Richards points out that faith not
only "justifies," faith also "vivifies." Paul explains it this
way:

> The life I live in the body, I live by faith in the
> Son of God, who loved me and gave himself for
> me (2:20b).

A Final Word on Works

Before we get too far along in this Bible study, we want
to clarify something about good works: They aren't in
themselves "bad." In Paul's the-
ology, there are three different
kinds of works. There is the "principle of works," which can't save
you. There are the "Mosaic works"
that were given to God's people
in order to give them rules to live
by. And there are the "good works" that God has saved us
to do (Ephesians 2:10). In response to modern-day Judaizers who say the "principle of faith" allows for a believer
to deliberately sin, we need to emphasize the good works
every Christian is called to do, not out of obligation to
the law or because we want to impress others, but because
Christ living in us compels us to do them. As Galatians
continues to unfold, Paul will develop this concept.

> We need to live our
> life the way Jesus
> would live our life if
> He had our life to live.
>
> —Dallas Willard

■ ▨ ▨

$\mathcal{S}$tudy the $\mathcal{W}$ord

1. Sharing a meal had great significance in the first century. What significance does it have in our time? Would you say that sharing meals together is more or less of a priority to families today than it was a generation ago? What does that say about our culture?

2. To get a sense of what God had taught Peter about removing the barriers between Jews and Gentiles, read Acts 10:9-15,28. What is the significance of this vision to Peter?

3. In what ways can you identify with Peter's reluctance to stand up to peer pressure? Describe a time when you were pressured to do something you knew wasn't right. What are some things you can do to fortify your spiritual backbone?

4. What are some things we do—either intentionally or unwittingly—to create divisions with one another rather than unity? Give an example of how an act of hypocrisy on the part of one person can cause someone else to act hypocritically.

5. Read Matthew 18:15-17. What benefits does this process offer to the offender? What benefits does it offer to the person who confronts? How well did Paul follow the advice Jesus offered?

6. Explain why the doctrine of justification by faith is the bedrock of Christianity. How does this doctrine distinguish Christianity from other belief systems?

7. What does it mean to you personally to be crucified with Christ?

   • in your conversion and call—

   • in your daily life—

We are justified by grace on the basis
of Christ's sacrifice.

—James Montgomery Boice

Paul Begins a Doctrinal Argument

In the first two chapters of his letter to the Galatians,
Paul gives the first of three major arguments to prove that
his gospel is true. He builds his case along three lines:

- He was appointed by Jesus as an apostle independent of the other apostles;

- His gospel message was confirmed by the other
  apostles; and

- He was compelled to oppose Peter, the head
  apostle, because he and the other hypocrites
  "were not following the truth of the gospel
  message" (2:14).

In the next two chapters of Galatians, Paul will continue
to argue that his gospel is true, only here his emphasis shifts
to the way God has delivered the Galatians—by means
of justification by faith in Jesus, not by works of the law.
Whereas the argument of Galatians 1 and 2 is *personal,* the
argument of Galatians 3 and 4 is *doctrinal.*

To reinforce this second major argument, Paul is going
to offer six proofs. Two of the proofs are in the section of
Scripture we are going to study next.

Chapter 6

Justified by Faith

Galatians 3:1-14

What's Ahead

- Foolish Galatians (3:1-5)
- True Descendants of Abraham (3:6-9)
- The Road Less Traveled (3:10-14)

From time to time you'll hear about someone you thought was pretty intelligent doing something really stupid. It could be a friend or a co-worker, but more often than not it's a celebrity. Maybe it's because they're in the limelight more than the rest of us mere mortals, but celebrities seem to fall prey to this "smart people doing dumb things" syndrome. At least you think they're smart, because they make all kinds of money and people adore them. But then they do something so ridiculously stupid that you literally yell at the television screen, "Have you lost your mind? What were you thinking?"

As far as Paul is concerned, the Galatians are like that. They are reasonably intelligent people, but they have done something incredibly stupid. So far in his letter Paul has been relatively cordial (if a little distant). Perhaps that's because so far the focus has been on him. Now that the spotlight is turning to the Galatians, Paul tells them what he really thinks.

Foolish Galatians (3:1-5)

You know what happened: The Galatians at one time embraced the truth of the gospel, but now they have adopted the view of the Judaizers, namely that the law—circumcision and dietary restrictions being just two examples—is necessary for justification. So Paul really cuts loose and gets personal, calling them "foolish Galatians!" We actually like Eugene Peterson's rendering in *The Message:* "You crazy Galatians!" Or how about this interpretation from J.B. Phillips:

> *Oh you dear idiots of Galatia...surely you can't be so idiotic!*

Heresy in Galatia

Too harsh? In our politically correct culture, we tend to be tolerant of people who bring different views to the table, even when it comes to the Bible. Especially in our small-group Bible studies, we accept the "perspectives" of people who think that one interpretation of a passage is as good as another. You can't criticize someone for saying something goofy, because it's their opinion, and an opinion has great value.

Well, that's fine if you're talking about matters that aren't essential to salvation, such as whether the Rapture is happening before or after the Tribulation, or whether or not it's okay for women to wear short hair (trust us, this is an issue in some circles). But when you're talking about the truth of the gospel, which is all about salvation, it isn't acceptable to bring heresy to the discussion (unless you are discussing why the heresy isn't true).

What Is Heresy?

When it comes to Bible doctrine, *heresy* is a belief or a chosen way of thinking and action that is different from or contradictory to the accepted belief of the revealed truth of Scripture. And just who determines what that "revealed truth" is, since there are often differing opinions on essential issues, such as justification by faith? The apostles were the foundational authority, since they were personally chosen by Jesus to establish His church. Beyond them, the early church "Fathers" articulated orthodox (correct) doctrinal positions on many issues that are essential to our faith—such as the nature of Christ, the reality of the triune God, and the inerrancy of Scripture.

The early church was plagued with three major heresies: the heresy of the Judaizers, which Paul is dealing with here; the Gnostic heresy, which denies the humanity of Christ; and the syncretistic heresy, which blends various beliefs and practices.

Clearly the Judaizers had introduced heresy to the Galatians, who were lapping it up like ice cream (or whatever tasty treat they had back then). Paul has no tolerance for this nonsense, because the person and work of Christ are at stake, not to mention the salvation of the Galatians. So he calls these nincompoops "foolish, crazy idiots."

Paul then uses a striking illustration. He says that "the meaning of Jesus Christ's death was made as clear to you as if you had seen a picture of his death on the cross" (3:1). That's how they were justified, not because of their works, but because of the atoning work of Christ. Nothing could be clearer.

The Proof Is in the Power

If there's one "sign" or indicator of the new birth, it's the presence of the Holy Spirit. All those who put their trust in Christ for salvation receive the Holy Spirit. In fact, the Holy Spirit is the one who "baptizes" us into the body of Christ (1 Corinthians 12:13). He is "God's guarantee that he will give us the inheritance he promised" (Ephesians 1:14). The Galatians received the Holy Spirit, a sure sign of their salvation.

In his first of six proofs showing that the Galatians have been justified by faith and not the law, Paul argues from the Galatians' own experience with the Holy Spirit. He asks them if they received the Spirit by the works of the law or by trusting in Christ by faith. He then looks at three aspects of their experience:

- *Reception of the Spirit* (3:2). Paul takes his readers back to the roots of their spiritual experience to remind them that the beginning of their faith was a gift of God's Spirit, not a result of anything they did.

- *Maturity in the Spirit* (3:3). Not only is the beginning a gift of the Spirit, but progress toward spiritual maturity is also. The Judaizers had convinced the Galatians they could become "perfect" by doing good works. Maturing in the Spirit is not about doing good works. It's "letting the Holy Spirit guide your lives" (5:16).

- *Miracles by the Spirit* (3:5). God is in the miracle business, and He especially likes doing miracles in the lives of new believers (a changed life is a miracle). Those who live in the Spirit's power see miracles. Those who live in the power of their good works do not.

The bottom line for Paul is this: The Galatians began their lives being justified by their faith, and the sign that Christ is living His life in them is the presence and the power of the Holy Spirit. Why would they now choose to finish their lives in the power of the flesh?

True Descendants of Abraham (3:6-9)

In his second proof in this section, Paul does something really clever. He appeals to Abraham, considered the father of the nation of Israel. Abraham predates Moses, and therefore he precedes the law of Moses. Look at what Paul does here. He points out that Abraham lived before Moses, and he was saved *by faith* (Genesis 15:6). Isn't that beautiful? Take that, you Judaizers!

Paul quickly tells Abraham's story in 3:6-9:

- God made a promise to Abraham
- Abraham believed God
- God declared Abraham righteous because of his faith
- Therefore, the real children of Abraham—the ones who will receive the blessings promised to Abraham—aren't his *physical* descendants, but his *spiritual* descendants, who are those who also believe God by faith.

This is the essence of justification by faith. Just as God declared Abraham to be righteous because of his faith, God declares us to be "just in His sight" (another way of saying "not guilty") because of our *faith,* not our works. This is a legal declaration by God, whereby He puts the righteousness of Christ on us.

Spiritual No-Man's-Land

The Judaizers had convinced the Galatians that their identity as physical descendants of Abraham was enough to put them in good standing with God. The problem—and this unveils the true hypocrisy of the Judaizers—was that they did not welcome the

Gentile believers into their synagogues. After all, they were still Gentiles, even if they were trying to keep the Jewish law. Talk about being in no-man's-land! Originally the Galatians had turned to God from their pagan practices. Now they were embracing the Jewish culture and laws, but they weren't being accepted as Jews.

Christians today fall into the same trap. Initially they turn from their sinful ways and receive Christ by faith, but then they trade their identity as God's children for the identify offered by the dominant forces of the surrounding culture. But since they have already turned their backs on the culture, they aren't welcome. They're in spiritual no-man's-land. If this is where you find yourself today, you need to realize that you belong to Christ, not the world.

The Road Less Traveled (3:10-14)

Christ has always offered the narrow road. He's never been the popular way to God for one simple reason: You don't have to work to get there. Every other religion ever devised by humankind has "works" as the centerpiece. Want to get to heaven, or achieve perfect consciousness, or find peace in the afterlife? Do good stuff. Pile up the brownie points. Do all you can to be a good person. Follow a long list of rules and regulations.

Only Christianity, with Jesus as the centerpiece, has this message: If you want to get into a right relationship with God, if you want eternal life, if you want to get to heaven, if you want to count for something in this life—you must put your trust in Jesus. Accept by faith what He has already done. That's it. That's the road less traveled.

The well-traveled road is the road of works. That's the road the Judaizers were recommending, mainly because it was the road their ancestors had taken for centuries. But as Paul skillfully points out, this creates a big problem, because anyone who doesn't keep all of the law is cursed.

Paul piles on Scripture after Scripture—quoting from the Book of the Law and the Prophets—to prove that the law can only condemn, not justify and save:

> *Cursed is anyone who does not affirm and obey the terms of these instructions* (Deuteronomy 27:26).

> *The righteous will live by their faithfulness to God* (Habakkuk 2:4).

> *If you obey my decrees and my regulations, you will find life through them* (Leviticus 18:5).

> *Anyone who is hung is cursed in the sight of God* (Deuteronomy 21:23).

Jesus was hanged on a tree, not because He was cursed, but because He took our curse on Himself. Jesus redeemed us—literally He rescued us from the curse—giving us the blessing promised to Abraham as evidenced by the Holy Spirit (3:14). The only way to escape the curse is not by our work, but by His!

What It Means to Be Redeemed

When Paul uses the word *redeemed* to describe what Jesus does for us, he is drawing upon a very well-known image of the first century. The word was used when someone purchased a slave for the purpose of freeing them. Jesus purchased our freedom when He died on the cross. When we believe in Jesus by faith and trust Him as Lord and Savior, we are redeemed from the slavery of the law and sin.

■ ▣ ▣

Study the Word

1. List three doctrinal issues that are not essential for salvation. Have any of these caused divisions in the church?

2. List three doctrinal issues that are essential for salvation. Have any of these brought the church together?

3. Give an example of a twenty-first-century version of each of these first-century heresies:

   • The heresy of the Judaizers

   • The Gnostic heresy

   • The syncretistic heresy

4. One of Paul's proofs for justification by faith is based on the Galatians' experience with the Holy Spirit:

- reception of the Spirit
- maturity in the Spirit
- miracles by the Spirit

Explain how a believer can know through these experiences that he or she has been saved by faith.

5. It is not uncommon for someone to profess belief in Christ as Savior, and then after a time slip back into the culture's mold. Why does this happen? What can a mature Christian do to help a new believer keep and develop his or her identity as a child of God?

6. Why do you think the road of God's grace and faith is so much less traveled than the road of works?

7. What is the "curse" Paul talks about in 3:10? Why was it necessary for Jesus to take this curse on Himself?

No man has ever appreciated the gospel until
the law has first revealed him to himself. It is
only against the inky blackness of the night sky
that the stars begin to appear, and it is only
against the dark background of sin and
judgment that the gospel shines forth.

—*John R.W. Stott*

God's Will

Bruce is a lawyer (don't hold that against him), and one
of his specialties in the practice of law is setting up wills
for people. In legal terms, a will is a statement that tells
the court what should be done with a person's property
after that person has died. Often you hear the term *will*
coupled with *testament,* as in *last will and testament.* A testament is a covenant or agreement. Together, the words *will
and testament* mean that legally, the governing authorities
agree to carry out the terms of the will, but only after the
person who made the will dies. At that point, nothing can
be added to the will or taken away.

Did you know that God has left us a will? This is what
Paul is telling the Galatians in this next section. God left
His last will and testament to Abraham, which means He
left it to us, too, as Abraham's spiritual descendants. And
nothing can be added to the will or taken away from the
will. Do you know why? Because the One who made the
will died.

Chapter 7

The Promise and the Law

Galatians 3:15-29

What's Ahead

- ■ The Promise Is Greater Than the Law (3:15-18)
- ■ So Why Was the Law Given? (3:19-25)
- ■ We Are One in Christ Jesus (3:26-29)

*P*aul has just explained that the only legitimate children of Abraham are those who are his spiritual descendants, having received the blessing God promised to Abraham through faith. Now Paul explains the nature of the promise and why the promise—in effect, God's will and testament—can never be revoked. This is the third proof for justification by faith alone.

The Promise Is Greater Than the Law (3:15-18)

The wonderful truth that emerges in this proof is that we do not have a relationship with God based on works (represented by the law of Moses), but on faith (represented by the promise made to Abraham). You see, the Judaizers were arguing that since the law came after the promise made to Abraham, it replaced the promise. But Paul makes it clear that God's promise is irrevocable. This is God's will, and it can't be changed once the maker of the will has died.

But God didn't die, did He? No, God didn't die, but Jesus, who is equal to God in every way, did. As Paul writes in his letter to the Philippians,

> *You must have the same attitude that Christ Jesus had. Though he was God, he did not think of equality with God as something to cling to. Instead, he gave up his divine privileges; he took the humble position of a slave and was born as a human being. When he appeared in human form, he humbled himself in obedience to God and died a criminal's death on a cross* (Philippians 2:5-8).

In effect, the promise God made to Abraham—His last will and testament—was ratified when Jesus died on the cross (Hebrews 9:16-28).

The Nature of the Promise

So just exactly what is this promise God made to Abraham? Paul explains that it involves Abraham's "seed" (3:16), or his descendants. Now, the Jewish people traditionally took this at face value to mean that all of the physical descendants of Abraham were inheritors of this blessing. But Paul puts the word *seed* into a messianic context, so that it refers to a single descendant of Abraham (referred to as "child" in the New Living Translation). Obviously, this "child" is Christ—God's only Son.

The Law Does Not Overturn the Promise

God made His promise to Abraham around 2000 BC. More than four centuries later (430 years to be exact), God gave the law to Moses (we'll find out why God did this in a moment). Because this new agreement came after God's promise to Abraham, the Judaizers reasoned that it was attached to the original promise as a condition.

But this cannot be, because God's original promise—His last will and testament, as put in force by death—cannot be annulled, modified, changed, or revoked. The Mosaic covenant is clearly distinct from—not linked to—the Abrahamic covenant. God has not gone back on His promise. It's still in effect today, having been ratified by the death of Jesus on the cross. The bottom line is that every person who looks to the crucified Christ for salvation by faith, apart from any good works, receives the blessing of eternal life, which is what God promised to Abraham.

So Why Was the Law Given? (3:19-25)

Paul does us a big favor and answers the question that was probably on the mind of every Galatian (no doubt the question is on your mind, too): If it's so useless, why was the law given? If the law can't save us and make us right with God, what purpose does it serve? Great questions! (We thought you'd never ask.) Paul answers them by giving both the negative and the positive purposes of the law.

The Negative Purpose of the Law

There are two negative purposes for the law. These applied when God gave the law to Moses, and they apply today:

1. *The law was given to show people how guilty they are.* The law provides an objective standard by which violations (sins) are measured. In order for sinners to know how sinful they really are, God gave them the law. You can relate this to every law on the books

today. Laws exist to provide an objective standard by which everyone is measured.

Characteristics of the Law

Paul explains that the law had conditions. First, it had a time limit; it was in effect only until Christ came. Second, it didn't give people direct access to God; they needed a mediator. Third, the law depended on both parties of the agreement—God and His people—to keep the agreement. When Christ came, He became our mediator and gave us direct access to God. He activated God's promise, which depends *only on Him,* not on us.

2. *The law was given to show people that they are prisoners of sin.* The law demonstrates that all of us are sinners and under God's judgment. In this there is no distinction between Jews and Gentiles. The Bible says, "Everyone has sinned; we all fall short of God's glorious standard" (Romans 3:23). It doesn't help to keep the law because no one can keep it perfectly. No one can meet God's glorious (or perfect) standard. Paul is saying, "We're all sinners, and we don't qualify for, nor do we deserve, God's promise of eternal life. So the only way to receive God's promise is to believe in Jesus Christ" (3:22).

There Is No Conflict Between God's Law and God's Promise

As long as the law is given a *negative* role—showing us how guilty we are and showing us that we are prisoners of sin—there is no conflict between God's law and God's promise. It's only when the law is given a *positive* role—specifically, that good works can save us—that it is directly opposed to God's promise fulfilled in Christ. That's what was happening to the Galatians.

Paul had told them that the only way to enter into a right relationship with God was through the Spirit of Christ, and then the way to live in a right relationship with Christ was through the power of the Holy Spirit. The Judaizers were now telling them that the way to enter into a right relationship with God was through faith and good works, and then the way to live in a right relationship with Christ was to keep the law. Essentially the law was taking center stage and pushing Christ to the side. That's why Paul found it necessary to put the law back into its rightful place.

The Positive Purpose of the Law

The law wasn't all negative. Paul reminds his Jewish readers (including the Judaizers) that God gave them the law for two positive purposes:

1. *The law was given to keep them in protective custody.* The law was given to the Jews, not only to show them how guilty they were, but also to protect them until the promise to Abraham could be fulfilled in Christ. The first part of this purpose still applies to us today. The law is a reminder of God's perfect standard for all people—Jews and Gentiles alike. The second part of this purpose was for the Jews as a temporary system to guide their conduct. In effect, the law kept them in "protective custody" until Christ came.

2. *The law was given to be their guardian and teacher.* When we think of guardians and teachers, we imagine kindly instructors who encourage "give and take" between the teacher and student. Not so in Jewish culture. Back then a slave was assigned to each child

for the purpose of supervision. The supervisor was a strict disciplinarian who was responsible to give the child moral training and to protect him from the evils of society. In the same way, the law was given to give God's people moral training and to protect them from the evils of society.

Anyone—Jew or Gentile—who receives Christ by faith no longer needs to live under the supervisory control of the law. The law shows us that we need salvation, and God's grace in Jesus gives us that salvation.

We Are One in Christ Jesus (3:26-29)

People often accuse Christianity of being "intolerant." Nothing could be further from the truth. People who call themselves Christians can be intolerant, but the defining characteristic of faith in Jesus Christ is that the free gift of God's grace is available to all people. Through a series of brilliant images, Paul explains to the Galatians—and to us—just exactly what it means to be justified by faith.

- *We are children of God* (3:26). This was the highest title of honor given to a Jew. For us, it means God is our Father, who loves and cares for us as His own children.

- *We have been united with Christ in baptism* (3:27a). This refers to the baptism by the Holy Spirit into the body of Christ (1 Corinthians 12:13).

- *We have been made like him* (3:27b). We are in effect "clothed" with Christ (NIV). God literally puts the righteousness of Christ on us. As a result, our identities are now in Christ.

Clothed with Christ

In Roman society, when a young person came of age, he was given a special toga that symbolized he was a grown-up son. It also indicated he had full acceptance as a member of the family. The Galatian believers had put aside their old garments of the law and put on Christ's clothes of righteousness, giving them full acceptance as members of God's family. Now you know why Paul is so perplexed that the Galatians would want to put their crummy old clothing back on.

- *We are one in Christ Jesus* (3:28). This is at the core of the message of Galatians. In Jesus, there is no longer Jew or Gentile (there are no racial barriers); there is no longer slave or free (there are no social or class barriers); and there is no longer male or female (there are no gender barriers). Anything we do that contributes to any kind of racial, social, or gender superiority contradicts the truth of the gospel message.

- *We are true children of Abraham* (3:29). We are the heirs and the recipients of all the promises God gave to Abraham. The original promise God gave to Abraham (Genesis 12:3) was intended for anyone who receives Christ by faith.

So there you have it. God's last will and testament. How are you feeling by now? Do you feel a sense of pride—that you really deserve all of the promises God has given you in Christ Jesus? Or do you have a sense of deep humility? Are you tempted to add anything else to what Christ has already accomplished for you, or are you eternally grateful that His work on the cross did for you what you could never do for yourself? We think we know your answers to these questions, and we suspect they are the same as ours.

■ ■ ■

Study the Word

1. Explain how the death of Jesus "ratified" God's last will and testament (see Hebrews 9:16,27-28). Why is there no forgiveness without the shedding of blood (see Hebrews 9:22)?

2. Why did Paul put the word *seed* into a messianic context? What are the implications of this seed for the Jews? For the Gentiles?

3. Why wasn't the Mosaic covenant (or promise) attached as a condition of God's original promise to Abraham? Why is it so important for us that God's original promise is still in effect?

4. A law—whether you're talking about the law of Moses or a law in our society—is essentially an

agreement between the one who makes the law and those who are asked to observe the law. Explain why a law depends on both parties of the agreement to keep the agreement. What happens when the law is broken? In spiritual terms, what has Christ done for us with respect to God's law?

5. Do you agree that human beings are incapable of keeping God's law? Why or why not? What happens when the law is given a positive role? Why is this directly opposed to God's promise?

6. Expand on what it means to you personally to be clothed with Christ. List at least three benefits.

7. Does the church today look like the community Paul describes in 3:28? If not, why? What kinds of things do we do to erect barriers between those who are clothed with Christ? How can we begin to tear down these barriers?

Christ's love is a love without angles, a
love that asks nothing in return...this is
the quality that redeems.

—*David Wilkerson*

The Family of God

The family is the most enduring of all human institutions. Relationships can come and go—even friendships sometimes falter—but family is forever. It's no coincidence that the concept of the family is woven throughout Scripture. God created the family when He created Adam and Eve. He established the Jewish people (known as the children of Israel) as a family for His Son, Jesus, whose human ancestry can be traced back to Abraham (Matthew 1:1-17). In the New Testament, believers are part of the family of God. God is our heavenly Father (Ephesians 3:14), and we are His sons and daughters (2 Corinthians 6:18).

In this next section, where Paul offers his fourth proof to show that we are justified before God by faith and not by works, he continues to use the metaphor of the family—in particular children and heirs—to describe our relationship to God through Christ.

Chapter 8

From Slavery to Freedom

Galatians 4:1-11

What's Ahead

- Christ Came to Buy Our Freedom (4:1-7)
- Don't Become Slaves Again (4:8-11)

*I*n addition to setting up wills for people, Bruce helps put together trusts. Often the trusts are established for people who desire to protect their money upon their death. Sometimes the trusts are set up for minors in order to protect their interests until they are "of age." When a trust is completed for a child, the money actually belongs to the child, but the child can't use the money until he or she reaches a predetermined age (usually 18 or 21). Until that time, the child can't spend what legally belongs to him or her.

It is this second purpose of a trust that Paul has in mind here in the first part of Galatians 4. A minor in the first century was no different than a minor in the twenty-first century. Just like today, a first-century son who was an heir to his father's fortune was treated as fully dependent. In effect, he was no better than a slave. He had to obey his guardian until he came of age.

Christ Came to Buy Our Freedom (4:1-7)

Paul jumps to the obvious parallel between a minor child, who is no better than a slave, and someone who was "under the law" before Christ came. In effect he was a slave to "the basic spiritual principles of this world" (4:3). For a Jew, that meant slavery to the law. For the Gentile, that meant slavery to pagan (or godless) belief systems—or as Larry Richards puts it, to the "basic principles which operate in our lost world." The bottom line is that before Christ came, *all* people were enslaved to sin.

When the Right Time Came (4:4)

Sometimes people wonder why Jesus came to earth when He did. Only God knew it was the perfect time, and when we look back with the advantage of hindsight, we can see what Paul means when he writes, "When the right time came, God sent his Son" (4:4). Here are just three reasons why this was the right time:

- The Roman government and military had conquered most of the known world, creating peace between nations, enabling people to travel without restriction. This meant that missionaries like the apostle Paul could easily move from region to region without visas or passports.

- The Romans had built a very sophisticated transportation system throughout their vast empire (this is where the phrase "All roads lead to Rome" comes from). This meant that the Christian missionaries could travel in a very efficient manner.

- Even though the Romans were in charge of the government and transportation systems, the culture was still largely influenced by the Greeks. In fact, Greek was the common language of the Roman world. This meant that the early Christians could speak, preach, and write in a language that just about everyone could understand. In fact, the original New Testament writings were in Greek.

Not only was Jesus born at the right time, but He was also born with the right credentials. Paul writes that Jesus was "born of a woman," meaning that He was not only fully God, but also fully human. And Jesus was "subject to the law." This means that He not only fulfilled the law by keeping it perfectly, but He also paid its curse (Matthew 5:17).

God Sent Jesus to Buy Our Freedom (4:5)

All of humanity was in the slave market of sin, and by His death, Jesus paid the debt and purchased our freedom. This ultimate sacrifice paved the way for God to adopt us as "his very own children" (4:5). When you accept by faith the work of Jesus on your behalf, that's what happens. You transition from being a minor child, subject to the law and sin (and no better than a slave), and become a full-grown child of God. You "come of age," qualifying you to receive your spiritual inheritance. You have full and direct access to the resources of God in Christ Jesus (Philippians 4:19).

What It Means to Be Redeemed

When Paul writes that God sent Christ to "buy freedom for us who were slaves," he is talking about Christ's act of redemption. The word *redeem* simply means to "pay off." God created the human race to be in fellowship with Him, but because of our disobedience, we became enslaved to sin and to Satan and therefore separated from God. We incurred a debt of sin we could not pay. God sent Christ to "pay off" our debt of sin. That's why Christ is called "the Redeemer."

God Has Sent the Spirit of His Son into Your Hearts (4:6)

Not only did God send His Son, He also sent the Holy Spirit as a guarantee of, or "down payment" on, God's promised inheritance. Here's how Paul explains it in his letter to the Ephesians:

> *The Spirit is God's guarantee that he will give us the inheritance he promised and that he has purchased us to be his own people* (Ephesians 1:14).

Because of the presence of the Holy Spirit in your life, you have direct access to God through prayer. Think of it! God is your Father. You are no longer a slave to the "basic principles which operate in our lost world." You are God's grown-up child, and you have every right to call Him "Abba Father." It's like a child saying, "Daddy." Such an intimate relationship is possible only through the Holy Spirit, not through the law.

Galatians 4:6 is significant for another reason. It shows that all three persons of the Godhead—God the Father, God the Son, and God the Holy Spirit—are involved in your salvation: God the Father *authored* the plan of salvation, Jesus the Son *accomplished* the plan of salvation, and the Holy Spirit *applies* the plan of salvation.

Don't Become Slaves Again (4:8-11)

Paul is worried. He has explained to the Galatians in every possible way that they are free in Christ. He is sure of his gospel message:

- Through faith alone in Christ alone we have a relationship with God that we would never have through works;
- We have been redeemed from the slave market of sin; and
- We are no longer obligated to follow the "weak and useless spiritual principles of this world" (4:9).

And yet there seems to be a problem. The Galatians are "trying to earn favor with God" by what they do or don't do "on certain days or months or seasons or years" (4:10).

The Galatians were under the influence of the Judaizers—we know that—and evidently they were observing certain days on the Mosaic calendar in order to find favor with God. Now there's nothing wrong with setting aside certain days to remember what God has done for us, but when these remembrances are done in order to gain brownie points with God, then it's not right. It's like trying to add to our faith, which is what the Galatians were doing.

Even worse, they were embracing some of the "spiritual principles of this world." Some commentators see this as a reference to the "elemental" principles or spirits of the universe, such as the elements of earth, air, fire, and water. Does this sound familiar? There is a tendency among people who don't know God personally to worship the things God made (the creation) rather than God (the Creator). Paul writes in Romans,

> *Instead of worshiping the glorious, ever-living God, they worshiped idols made to look like mere people and birds and animals and reptiles* (Romans 1:23).

It's Good to Be Green Unless...

It's very fashionable (and probably a pretty good thing) to have great respect for the earth. Environmentalists aren't known as "tree huggers" any more. These days they are more likely to be called "Green," and everyone seems to be jumping on the environmental bandwagon. We don't have a problem with that. In fact, Christians should be leading the pack when it comes to being good "stewards," or managers, of the natural resources God has given us. But when saving the whales supersedes worshiping the Creator of the whales, something has gone wrong.

The bottom line is, there's nothing you can add to your faith. Yes, God is pleased when you display those qualities and do those things that help others and give Him glory. But they don't motivate or inspire God to love you any more than He already does. Your good deeds—no matter how good—add nothing to your faith. However, as we have said previously, God wants you to do good works—not because they add something to your faith, but because doing them fulfills the purpose He has for you here on earth (Ephesians 2:10).

Besides, as Paul is going to tell us later in this letter, any good you do comes from God anyway. It's only as you live by the Spirit's power that you can produce those character qualities that honor and glorify God.

Why Does Paul Fear for the Galatians?

In the last verse of this section, Paul writes, "I fear for you. Perhaps all my hard work with you was for nothing" (4:11). Does this mean Paul fears that the Galatians are in danger of "losing" their salvation? Though some have made a case for this view, this doesn't seem to be what Paul is implying. For one thing, he would have been more explicit. Instead, he is simply expressing frustration that his hard work seems to mean very little to the Galatians. As you read the rest of the letter, and then compare Paul's other writings to other churches, you will see that Paul is confident "that God, who began the good work within you, will continue his work until it is finally finished on the day when Christ Jesus returns" (Philippians 1:6).

■ ■ ■

$\mathcal{S}$tudy the $\mathcal{W}$ord

1. Explain the parallel between a child being subject to a guardian and all people being in slavery to the basic principles that operate in our lost world.

2. Why did God send Jesus at the time He did? In what ways was Jesus born with the right credentials? Why was it necessary for Jesus to be subject to the law?

3. Name three benefits of being a full-grown child of

God. Just because you are full grown, are you necessarily mature? How does a child of God become spiritually mature?

4. Explain the concept of *redemption* as it applies to the Christian life.

5. What role does the Holy Spirit play in your life...
   - in your salvation (John 3:5-8; 1 Corinthians 12:13)?

   - in your assurance of salvation (Ephesians 1:14)?

   - in your spiritual maturity (John 16:13-15; Romans 8:26-27)?

6. In what ways did God *author* the plan of salvation? How did Jesus *accomplish* the plan of salvation? How does the Holy Spirit *apply* the plan of salvation?

7. List some ways we try to find favor with God even after He has saved us. How do these things keep us from maturing as God's children?

You should follow my example, just as I follow Christ.

—Paul

A Soft Heart and a Brilliant Mind

There's no question that Paul is a skilled writer. As he continues to develop his brilliant argument for justification by faith, he has come at the Galatians from four different angles:

- The Galatians' own experience of receiving the Holy Spirit proves that salvation comes by faith;

- Jews and Gentiles alike become spiritual descendants of Abraham when they believe, as Abraham did, in the God who justifies by faith;

- God's promise to Abraham was not changed by the law; and

- Jews and Gentiles alike have been set free from the law and are now full-grown children of God.

Now Paul takes a new approach, and it's very personal. In his fifth proof for justification by faith, Paul appeals to the wonderful and mutually trusting relationship he had with the Galatians when he first taught them—and they first received—the true gospel message. By comparison, Paul reminds them that the false teachers had selfish motives. They were looking out for themselves, not the Galatians. As you study this section, take special note of Paul's emotions, which show he has a soft heart as well as a brilliant mind.

Chapter 9

Paul Gets Personal

Galatians 4:12-20

$\mathcal{W}$hat's $\mathcal{A}$head

■ Paul Appeals to His Relationship with the Galatians (4:12-16)

■ Paul Exposes the Motives of the Judaizers (4:17-18)

■ The Art of Spiritual Formation (4:19-20)

$\mathcal{P}$eople don't care how much you know until they know how much you care. Have you found that to be true? We sure have. Especially when it comes to talking about God and the reality of His plan to save us through Jesus Christ. The facts alone aren't enough for most people. You may be able to tell others about God in a way that makes perfect sense to you, but if you just recite the facts about God without sharing something of yourself, your words may fall on deaf ears. People need to know that you love them and care about them in a way that shows your heart before they will listen to the words of your message.

Paul Appeals to His Relationship with the Galatians (4:12-16)

Notice how Paul now addresses the Galatians. He calls them "Dear friends," which is quite a contrast from "foolish Galatians." At this point Paul isn't instructing or rebuking. Paul is *pleading*. He is asking the Galatians from the depths of his heart to imitate him, to live as he does "in freedom from these things" (4:12). At first glance this may seem like a prideful appeal. Normally, if you want to win somebody over on a personal level, you don't say, "Be like me!" You would be more likely to point to someone else. In Paul's case, an appeal to "be like Christ" would seem more appropriate.

Be Like Paul

Certainly Paul wants the Galatians to be like Jesus. But there is a reason for his seemingly self-centered approach, and it won't be the first time he will hold himself up as an example. Later, he will advise the Corinthians,

> *You should imitate me, just as I imitate Christ* (1 Corinthians 11:1).

And in his letter to the church at Philippi, he will give this advice:

> *Dear brothers and sisters, pattern your lives after mine* (Philippians 3:17).

In all of these letters, Paul is saying, "Be like me." He takes this approach, not because he thinks so highly of himself, but because he knows that the best way for a person to be drawn to Christ is to see Christlike qualities in others. It's just human nature to look to other people for inspiration and motivation. How often have you been encouraged to read a book or see a movie because someone you respect recommended it? How often have you been motivated to exercise or take up a hobby or try something new because a person you can identify with has already done it? If you're like us, the answer is, "Lots of times."

Now, becoming a committed disciple of Christ is a lot more important than reading a book, watching a movie, or getting in shape, but the principle is the same. We need models and heroes as examples to motivate us to do the right thing—in this case, follow Christ more fully. Paul knows this. So he appeals to his past relationship with the Galatians, who embraced him warmly on his first visit. He reminds them that he became like "you Gentiles" when he abandoned the law, recognized his sin, and turned to Jesus by faith. Paul's emotions pour out as he pleads with his friends to now become like him and embrace God's grace rather than defect to legalism.

What Kind of Illness Did Paul Have?

Paul commends the Galatians for receiving him on his first visit, especially since he was sick at the time. In fact, Paul reminds them, his sickness was "revolting" to them (4:14 TLB). So what was wrong with Paul? And is this the same as the "thorn in the flesh" Paul later refers to in 2 Corinthians 12:7? Bible scholars have offered various theories about Paul's illness. Some have suggested malaria, a common disease of that time, while others have speculated that Paul had epilepsy. Martin Luther thought Paul was referring to the injuries he had received because of constant physical persecution. The most common conclusion is that Paul had poor eyesight, perhaps an eye disease of some kind. This seems to fit Paul's statement about the Galatians' depth of commitment to him: "In those days, I know you would gladly have taken out your own eyes and given them to replace mine if that would have helped me" (4:15).

The Joy Is Gone

Even though they once welcomed Paul with open arms, the Galatians' commitment to Paul seems to be a thing of the past, along with the joy they all experienced together. If you've ever been part of a group of Christians who love the Lord and one another, then you know what Paul is talking about when he laments, "What has happened to all your joy?" (4:15). Whether you've experienced fellowship in a small group at church, or among your own family members, you know the special joy that comes from having a common bond, especially when that bond is built around the Lord. Now Paul is saying that without their spiritual connection, the joy is gone.

Joy comes from a spiritual source; it is deep and abiding. Happiness, which is what everybody wants, is fleeting. It depends on circumstances and the actions of others. Joy comes from within and is produced when we understand that Jesus is the source of our peace and our contentment no matter what the circumstances. It's why Paul could write to the Philippian church from prison, "Whatever happens, my dear brothers and sisters, rejoice in the Lord" (Philippians 3:1).

Paul asks his former friends in Galatia what has happened to their joy. Of course, it's a rhetorical question. Paul knows what has happened. The Judaizers have convinced the Galatians that Paul is not a legitimate apostle and that his gospel is deficient because it excludes the law. Rather than embrace him, the Galatians have shunned him, treating him like an enemy because he is preaching the truth of grace.

Paul Exposes the Motives of the Judaizers (4:17-18)

While Paul came to the Galatians with pure motives and true love—he wanted only what was best for them—

the Judaizers came to the Galatians under a false pretense. They weren't looking out for the Galatians. They were anxious to gain their approval (the NIV says they were "zealous" to win them over), and the way they did that was to shut them off from Paul in order to strengthen their own cause.

$\mathcal{M}$isplaced $\mathcal{Z}$eal

According to Scot McKnight, Paul is using the word *zeal* here negatively to describe an emotion of "jealousy and intensity" that tries to get something done, often through violence. In the first century there was a "party of Zealots" among the Jews, which worked to overthrow Rome through violence, but it's unlikely that the Judaizers in Galatia were part of the Zealot movement. What is clear is that the Judaizers were nationalistic in their zeal, in that the central feature of their legalistic message was Israel and the law. Paul says it's fine to be zealous for a cause, provided you are "eager to do good things" (4:18). Being zealous for God is good; being zealous for something that separates people from God and from each other is not good.

The Art of Spiritual Formation (4:19-20)

Until this section of his letter, Paul has been tough. Now Paul gets tender. He addresses the Galatians as "my dear children" (4:19) and openly agonizes over their lack of spiritual growth. Paul longs for Christ to be "developed" (NLT) and "formed" (NIV) in them. He wants so much for these spiritual children to grow into mature Christians, whose very lives are conformed to the character of Christ. The idea that Paul wants the Galatians to imitate him ties directly to this concept of spiritual formation, which takes place when we incorporate the character of Christ into our lives. This theme runs throughout Paul's letters:

> *Don't copy the behavior and customs of this world, but let God transform you into a new person by changing the way you think. Then you will learn to know God's will for you, which is good and pleasing and perfect* (Romans 12:2).

> *Clothe yourself with the presence of the Lord Jesus Christ. And don't let yourself think about ways to indulge your evil desires* (Romans 13:14).

> *Let the Spirit renew your thoughts and attitudes. Put on your new nature, created to be like God— truly righteous and holy* (Ephesians 4:23-24).

> *Don't be drunk with wine, because that will ruin your life. Instead, be filled with the Holy Spirit* (Ephesians 5:18).

Becoming like Christ doesn't happen automatically. As these verses advise, we must take responsibility for our spiritual formation by...

- letting God transform us;
- clothing ourselves with Jesus;
- putting on the new nature God has given us; and
- inviting the Holy Spirit to fill and control us.

We can't do this ourselves. As Paul writes elsewhere, the only way we can be free from a life dominated by sin is "in Jesus Christ our Lord" (Romans 7:25).

If you have trusted in Jesus Christ alone by faith alone, you have been redeemed from the slave market of sin. That's your *position* in Christ. But your everyday *experience* in Christ depends on a moment-by-moment willingness on your part to allow the Holy Spirit to control you. Paul is going to develop this theme in Galatians 5, but before he does that he has one more illustration from the Old Testament that will complete his argument for justification by faith. We'll consider that in the next chapter.

■ ■ ■

Study the Word

1. Would you be comfortable with inviting another believer to be like you? Why or why not? Why is it important that you live your life in such a way that others will want to follow your example?

2. Name at least three spiritual heroes or role models you have in your life. What qualities in each of these people are you trying to imitate? (By the way, your role models could be living right now, but it's not necessary.)

3. Regardless of the kind of illness or physical problem Paul had, do you think this hindered or helped Paul?

Think of a time when you had a physical problem. How did this affect your relationship with Christ?

4. Why do most people seek happiness rather than joy? What is the net effect when someone spends their time trying to be happy? What's the best way to shift your efforts from trying to find happiness to seeking joy?

5. Give an example from contemporary culture of someone who is zealous for something that separates them from God. Is it possible for a Christian to develop this kind of misplaced zeal? How?

6. What are the three indicators that the character of Christ is being formed in your life? (Refer to Romans 12:2; 13:14; Ephesians 4:23-24.)

7. What's the best way to take responsibility for your spiritual formation? What kind of spiritual "disciplines" do you need to practice in order for this to happen?

8. Describe the difference between your *position* in Christ and your *experience* in Christ.

Make the Kingdom of God your primary concern.

—*Jesus*

*W*ho's *W*ho

When you attend a live performance of a play or musical, you generally receive a program that helps you follow the story. The program contains, among other things, a summary of the plot, a description of the setting, and a list of the cast of characters. As we enter this next section, where Paul gives the Galatians the sixth proof to support his argument that we are justified by faith, he tells a familiar story from the Old Testament, involving no fewer than five characters. They are...

Abraham   Called by God to be the father of a great nation. God promised Abraham a son and countless descendants, and that his offspring would bless the whole world.

Sarah   Abraham's wife and the mother of Isaac. Doubted that God could give her a son at her age.

Hagar   Servant of Abraham and Sarah, and the mother of Ishmael.

Ishmael   Abraham's son with Hagar. For 13 years Abraham thought Ishmael was the fulfillment of God's promise.

Isaac   Son of Abraham and Sarah, and first descendant in the fulfillment of God's promise to Abraham.

The plot summary will follow as Paul takes this familiar story and uses it to teach the Galatians (and us) an important lesson.

Chapter 10

A Story for the Ages

Galatians 4:21-31

What's Ahead

- The Story of Isaac and Ishmael (4:21-23)
- The Allegorical Interpretation (4:24-27)
- The Application (4:28-31)

Reading and studying the Bible is one of the most important things you can do in your Christian life. The Bible is God's personal, inspired message to you. It tells you about Him and His plan to bring you into a right relationship with Him. Furthermore, the Bible teaches you what is true and prepares you to do "every good work" that God wants you to do (2 Timothy 3:16).

You will get something out of Scripture every time you read it. At the same time, there is great value to using sound methods of interpretation in your Bible study. When you bring out the meaning of a Bible passage, you are engaging in interpretation. The goal of interpreting the Bible should be to apply the meaning of what you learn to your life. To do this, you first begin with the meaning of the text in its context, and then you move to the application in your present-day context.

This is what Paul is doing in this section. He takes a story that is familiar to the Galatians (especially the Jewish Christians) and brings out the meaning by turning it into an allegory in order to teach an important spiritual principle. Let's see how he does this.

The Story of Isaac and Ishmael (4:21-23)

Before he gives a quick summary of the story, Paul asks the Galatians (who want to live under the law) a sarcastic question: "Do you know what the law actually says?" (4:21). It would be like someone telling you, "I want to live under a dictatorship," to which you would reply, "Do you know what a dictatorship really is?"

Obviously, the Galatians don't know what the law really says, so Paul reviews the story of Isaac and Ishmael in order to tell them. Ishmael was the son of Abraham and Hagar, a slave woman. As Paul explains, this was a "human attempt" to produce an heir. It showed that Sarah didn't believe God could make good on His promise, so she took matters into her own hands. Since she was 90 years old and far beyond her childbearing years, she convinced Abraham to have a child with Hagar.

The *New American Standard Bible* says that Ishmael was born "according to the flesh." The word *flesh* here means "not living according to the promise of God." Another way to say it is that "fleshly" = "unbelief." (Paul will develop the concept of "flesh" later in Galatians 5.)

Thankfully, Abraham believed God's promise that his wife would be able to conceive a child, and Sarah gave birth to Isaac. So here are these two sons, one born from a slave according to the flesh, and the other born free as God's fulfillment of His promise (4:23).

The Allegorical Interpretation (4:24-27)

With the facts of the story laid out, Paul then provides an interpretation through an allegory. Paul isn't saying the original events didn't really happen. He is simply using the story to bring out the spiritual meaning of the story (that's what an allegory does). Although the two births are historical events, the two women represent two covenants, or agreements:

- *Hagar, the slave woman, represents the old covenant*—the covenant of law—that God made with Moses on Mt. Sinai. This covenant corresponds to the earthly Jerusalem, which was the home base of the Judaizers and their legalism. Spiritual children of Hagar's son, Ishmael, are obligated to the law.

- *Sarah, the free woman, represents the new covenant*—the covenant of promise—that God made through Jesus. This covenant corresponds to the heavenly Jerusalem, which is the future home of all who trust in Christ alone by faith alone. Spiritual children of Sarah's son, Isaac, are acceptable to God because of faith.

Two Covenants, Two Ages, Two Kingdoms

This allegory, where the two mothers represent the two covenants, connects with other aspects of Paul's theology. Paul sees these two covenants corresponding to two "ages." There is the present age, the age of sin and the law, which Paul refers to as "this evil world in which we live" (1:4). In this age "we were slaves to the basic spiritual principles of this world" (4:3). This is an earthly kingdom ruled by Satan.

Then Christ came at "the right time" (4:4) to inaugurate the age of righteousness and grace. This age is sometimes called the "Messianic age" because here is where God sent Christ "to buy freedom for us who were slaves to the law, so that he could adopt us as his very own children" (4:5). By accepting the person and work of Jesus by faith, we have the opportunity to live in a heavenly kingdom of light ruled by Jesus.

Although we have been rescued from Satan's kingdom of darkness and been brought into Jesus' kingdom of light, the present evil age still exists. Even though we are covered by Christ's righteousness, we are still vulnerable to temptation and sin. Later, Paul will explain what it means to live as citizens of Christ's kingdom by letting the Holy Spirit control our lives.

The Application (4:28-31)

We said earlier that good Bible interpretation begins with the meaning of the text in its context and then moves to an application in the current-day context. This is exactly what Paul is doing. His application for his audience is that those who are "children of the promise"—that is, Abraham's spiritual children—are just like Isaac.

What about us? What's the application for those of us who are Abraham's spiritual children? As you study the Bible, you are able to bring the contexts together: the context of Abraham's day, the context of Paul's day, and the context of your day. These three contexts span more than 4000 years, yet the application is timeless and completely fresh. The application is the same for you as it was for the Galatians. If you have put your trust in Jesus Christ by faith, you are Isaac, the child of promise, not Ishmael, the child of unbelief.

Expect Persecution

Paul introduces the topic of persecution in 4:29. He writes, "You are now being persecuted by those who want you to keep the law." He compares this to the persecution Ishmael dished out to Isaac. What kind of persecution is Paul talking about? When you go to the account in Genesis, you find that Ishmael made fun of Isaac (see Genesis 21:9). Keeping in mind that Ishmael was a teenager and Isaac was about three years old, it might appear that the "persecution" amounted to little more than immature teasing. Actually, it was more than that. Ishmael was probably mocking Isaac. Still, is that persecution?

As Christians, we tend to think of persecution in the most extreme sense of the word, such as people being tortured or killed for their faith in Jesus. Certainly that is a harsh reality that existed in the first century and has continued unabated into our own time. But is that what Paul is referring to here in Galatians? As we said in chapter 9, it's unlikely that the Judaizers—"those who want us to keep the law"—were using violence against those who are born of the Holy Spirit. But they were probably mocking and ridiculing them, something that is tough to handle (just remember what it did to Peter).

What Kind of Persecution Can We Expect?

For those of us who are Christians living in the West, we can expect to be mocked and ridiculed rather than tortured and killed. In fact, if we aren't being mocked, ridiculed, and made fun of, then we probably aren't standing out as bold witnesses for Christ. If people aren't disapproving of what we are saying about

Jesus, then we aren't speaking up. That doesn't mean that we should make statements just to irritate or incite others, but if we are speaking the truth in love, we can expect vocal opposition. That's because "the message of the cross" sounds ridiculous to "those who are headed for destruction" (1 Corinthians 1:18).

Persecution in the form of opposition and ridicule shouldn't take us by surprise. Jesus said that those who do not trust in Him "hate the light and refuse to go near it for fear their sins will be exposed" (John 3:20). He also warned His followers that the world would hate them "because they do not belong to the world, just as I do not" (John 17:14).

Get Rid of the Troublemakers

Persecution can come from the outside, and it can also come from within. Just as Isaac was ridiculed by his half-brother, Ishmael, and just like the religious Judaizers were ridiculing those who followed Christ by faith, we can expect to be ridiculed and opposed by our spiritual "half-brothers," or what John Stott calls "the nominal church." According to Stott, the greatest enemies of the evangelical faith today are those in the church who want to preserve tradition and power. As Paul completes his allegory, he advises the Galatian believers to "get rid of" those who were causing trouble, just as Abraham and Sarah got rid of Ishmael and Hagar (Genesis 21:10). The lesson for us is that those who stand for the truth of the gospel need to deal with those in the church who are opposing them with a false gospel.

Expect an Inheritance

As Paul closes this section, he takes the Judaizers' own words and throws them back in their faces. The Judaizers had made a case for following the law as a way to get in good with God. In fact, the children of the slave woman, who are obligated to the law, will *not* share in the family inheritance. Only the children of the free woman, who are acceptable to God because of their faith, will receive God's inheritance.

◼ ◼ ◼

$\mathcal{S}$tudy the $\mathcal{W}$ord

1. Read 2 Timothy 3:16. Make a list of the spiritual benefits of reading God's Word.

2. What is the goal of Bible interpretation? What is the best way to accomplish this goal?

3. Sarah didn't believe God could make good on His promise, so she took matters into her own hands. What was the effect of her actions? Can you think of a time when you failed to trust God and instead took matters into your own hands? What happened?

4. Under the two columns below, list the characteristics of each description:

Old Covenant	**New Covenant**
This evil age in which we live	Age of righteousness and grace
Earthly kingdom ruled by Satan	Heavenly kingdom ruled by Jesus

5. What is the application of Paul's allegory for us?

6. Have you ever experienced any persecution for your faith in Christ? If not, what are you *not* doing that would cause people to mock or ridicule you for the cause of Christ?

7. How do you balance Paul's advice to "get rid of" troublemakers with Jesus' advice on how to handle someone who sins against you? (See Matthew 18:15-17.)

Freedom in Christ does not give us the right
to do as we please but the power and
ability to do as we ought.

—*Max Anders*

Defending Christian Freedom

We now come to the third of Paul's three arguments to prove that the gospel he is preaching is true. His first argument was laid out in Galatians 1 and 2. Here Paul defended his apostolic authority, showing that his message is from God, not men. His second argument was laid out in Galatians 3 and 4. Here Paul showed that God delivered the Galatians by means of justification by faith, not by works of the law. Now, beginning in Galatians 5 and continuing through the end of the letter, Paul presents his third argument: True deliverance from this present evil age and true freedom from the power of sin are possible only through Christ and the power of the Holy Spirit.

As we will see, Paul is defending Christian freedom, and this is huge. The Judaizers had argued that grace leads to sin. Paul is going to show that people who have been truly transformed by the grace of God through faith in Christ will indeed do those things God wants them to do—not because their works have merit, but because their works are evidence they are living in the power of the Holy Spirit.

Chapter 11

It Is for Freedom That Christ Set Us Free

Galatians 5:1-12

What's Ahead

- You Are Free, Now Stand Firm (5:1-6)
- Characteristics of False Teachers (5:7-12)

*I*t's one thing to be set free, and quite another to live that way. Imagine you have committed a serious crime and are sentenced to spend the rest of your life in prison. Then, for reasons unrelated to your behavior, you are pardoned by the governor, who has the authority to set you free. You don't deserve the pardon and you did nothing to bring it about, but you are shown mercy. So there you are, standing outside the prison walls, a free person. What do you do next? Do you go on a crime spree, believing the governor will pardon you again, or do you take responsibility for your life and live as a free person?

That's the point Paul is making here as he begins a new section. We were under a life sentence:

- prisoners of sin (3:22);
- guarded by the law (3:23); and
- slaves to the "basic spiritual principles of this world" (4:3).

But then Jesus Christ, who had the authority to pardon us, set us free:

- from this evil world in which we live (1:4); and
- from the "curse pronounced by the law" (3:13).

Here we are, standing outside the prison walls, free people. Do we go back to our old lives as prisoners of sin and slaves to this world, or do we take responsibility for ourselves and live as free people?

You Are Free, Now Stand Firm (5:1-6)

Why did Christ set us free? The NIV says it best: "It is for freedom that Christ has set us free" (5:1). Another way to say it would be this: Christ set us free so we could *be free*. He didn't set us free so we could once again become prisoners and slaves to this world. So why do we turn our back on what Jesus has done for us and return to a life of sin? And why do we think we can get back in God's good graces by trying to do good?

Paul's point here is that we need to live as free people. We need to "stand firm" (NIV). For the Galatians this means standing firm against the Judaizers, who want to enslave them to the law once again. For us it means standing firm against sin, legalism, and the world.

You Can't Stand Firm Alone

No matter how hard you "try" to stand firm against sin, legalism, and the world, you can't do it on your own. Paul gives us at least three ways we can and should stand firm:

- We need to stand firm in our faith (1 Corinthians 16:13);

- We need to stand firm with one another, fighting together for the truth of the gospel (Philippians 1:27); and

- We need to stand firm in the Lord, on whom our faith depends from start to finish (Philippians 4:1; Hebrews 12:2).

As far as the Galatians are concerned, Paul can see it coming. The Galatians are about to buy into the notion that circumcision will truly make them saved. Remember, to the Judaizers, circumcision was more than a physical procedure. It was a symbol that you had to have the right background and do everything your religion required in order for God to accept you.

Knowing this mind-set, Paul methodically lists four inevitable consequences of following this radical course of action:

1. *Christ will be of no benefit to you* (5:2). It is not because Christ is powerless, but because someone who depends on his own efforts for salvation rejects what Christ has already done.

2. *You must obey every regulation in the whole law of Moses* (5:3). Paul has made this point already, but he reviews it here to remind the Galatians that no one has ever done this and no one ever will—except for the sinless Christ.

3. *You have been cut off from Christ* (5:4). Talk about a graphic play on words! Those who submit to the "cutting" of circumcision to make themselves right with God are in effect cutting themselves off from the saving work of Christ.

4. *You have fallen away from God's grace* (5:4). Paul's warning here does not imply that those who have once received Christ by grace through faith will somehow "lose" their salvation. The issue is not *eternal security* but our *effective relationship* with Christ.

The Difference Between Eternal and Earthly Deliverance

The context of Galatians 5:1-12 makes it clear that Paul is writing to those who have been set free in Christ (5:1), but who must take responsibility to "live by the Spirit" (5:5a). Those who have "received by faith the righteousness God has promised" (5:5b) have experienced *eternal deliverance* from the *penalty of sin*. That's what it means to be justified by faith. However, those who rely on their own efforts to live the Christian life lose their *earthly deliverance* from the *power of sin*.

Stay Free

Having explained the consequences of getting "tied up again in slavery to the law," Paul now paints a contrasting picture beginning in 5:5:

> We who live by the Spirit eagerly wait to receive by faith the righteousness God has promised to us.

As Christians, we have already been rescued from the slave market of sin. We have been delivered eternally from the penalty of sin. But we still live in the "present evil age," where temptation and sin are ever present. So we have a choice. We can either stay free as we live "by the Spirit," or we can become enslaved again as we let our old sin nature control us. Here's how Paul explains it in Romans:

> *Do not let sin control the way you live; do not give in to sinful desires. Do not let any part of your body become an instrument of evil to serve sin. Instead, give yourselves completely to God, for you were dead, but now you have new life. So use your whole body as an instrument to do what is right for the glory of God. Sin is no longer your master, for you no longer live under the requirements of the law. Instead, you live under the freedom of God's grace* (Romans 6:12-14).

Already, but Not Yet

Theologians like to describe this condition of existing as free people in a sinful world as living in between "already" and "not yet." We have "already" been justified by Christ, but we are "not yet" living with Christ in heaven, where there will be no more sin. However, even though we are "not yet" living with Jesus in heaven, we are living in His spiritual kingdom, which was inaugurated at His first coming.

In Christ Jesus

Being "in Christ" means He has delivered us from sin eternally. But it also means Jesus delivers us from sin in our earthly existence—if we let the Holy Spirit control us and we do those things God wants us to do. If you're wondering what "those things" are, here's what Jesus has to say:

"You must love the LORD your God with all your heart, all your soul, and all your mind." This is the first and greatest commandment. A second is equally important: "Love your neighbor as yourself." The entire law and all the demands of the prophets are based on these two commandments (Matthew 22:37-40).

That's what Paul means when he speaks of "faith expressing itself in love" (5:6). When we place our faith in Christ Jesus, we are justified for eternity. But we have a responsibility to live for Christ daily in the power of the Holy Spirit by loving God and truly loving others. Paul is going to expand on this idea in the next section, but first he has a few parting shots for the Judaizers.

Characteristics of False Teachers (5:7-12)

In Galatians 4:30, Paul advised the Galatians to "get rid of" those false teachers who are telling them to add works to their salvation. Now Paul gives the Galatians some guidelines for spotting these troublemakers. In six verses Paul gives six characteristics of the Judaizers, vividly exposing the methodology of these false teachers. As you go through these, you will see that the tactics used by false teachers today are pretty much the same as they were nearly 2000 years ago.

1. *You were running the race so well. Who has held you back from following the truth* (5:7)? "Running the race" gives the verse a sports flavor, which Paul often uses. With the image of a race in mind, the next phrase describes a false teacher as one who interferes with a runner during a race. The Galatians were running their race well, but then the Judaizers hindered their

progress with heretical ideas. In a race, the one who interferes with another runner is disqualified. The same thing should happen to false teachers.

2. *It certainly isn't God, for he is the one who called you to freedom* (5:8). God will never hold us back from the truth. It is the false teachers, with their false ideas, who distract us and throw us off track. God promises to reward those who sincerely seek Him (Hebrews 11:6). False teachers draw attention to themselves rather than the truth.

3. *This false teaching is like a little yeast that spreads through the whole batch of dough* (5:9). It takes only one false teacher to affect and infect an entire church. And just like God would not accept yeast-filled bread as an offering in the Old Testament (Exodus 34:25), He will not accept doctrine that is infested with false teaching.

4. *I am trusting the Lord to keep you from believing false teachings. God will judge that person, whoever he is, who has been confusing you* (5:10). Clear and simple, false teachers cause trouble and create confusion. If you observe someone doing this in your church, chances are very good that he is distorting the truth of the gospel.

5. *If I were still preaching that you must be circumcised—as some say I do—why am I still being persecuted?* (5:11). One of the sure signs to Paul that the Judaizers are preaching a false gospel—and he is not—is that they are persecuting him. This is true today as well. One of the characteristics of false teachers is that they

spread lies and false rumors about spiritual leaders who preach the true gospel.

6. *I just wish that those troublemakers who want to mutilate you by circumcision would mutilate themselves* (5:12). Paul uses harsh language to make a very important point. False teachers will often insist on harsh practices or rituals. You may not find false teachers today pushing circumcision, but they will often insist that their followers cut themselves off from family and the church.

As you look at these characteristics, we don't want you to get paranoid and begin looking for false teachers under every pew or behind every curtain. But you need to be alert, and you need to know correct teaching in order to detect false teaching. The best way to do that is to study the Scriptures and immerse yourself in true teaching (2 Timothy 2:15), which comes from the teaching of God's word and the teaching of your spiritual leaders. As you take responsibility to study the Scriptures, God promises to help you understand His truth through the Holy Spirit:

> *We have received God's Spirit (not the world's spirit), so we can know the wonderful things God has freely given us* (1 Corinthians 2:12).

Staying free in Christ and standing firm in the truth isn't always easy, but it is something every Christian needs to do. Only we can't do it on our own. We need the power of the Holy Spirit released in our lives. As we move on to the next section of Galatians, Paul is going to tell us how to do that.

■ ■ ■

Study the Word

1. Since there is no benefit for us Christians (who are free in Christ) to return to our old lives as prisoners of sin, why do we do it? What's the enticement? Why do we think we can get back in God's good graces by trying to do good?

2. What is God's prescription for standing firm against legalism, sin, and the world?

3. What are the consequences of believing you must have the right background and do certain things in order for God to accept you?

4. Explain how the context of Galatians 5:1-12 makes it clear that Paul is addressing Christians here. Do

you believe Paul is saying that these Christians can "lose" their salvation? Why or why not?

5. Having "by faith the righteousness God has promised to us" means we have experienced eternal deliverance from the penalty of sin. On a practical level, how do we live with the earthly deliverance from the power of sin?

6. What does it mean to live in between "already" and "not yet"? How does this knowledge help you?

7. Have you personally encountered any of the six characteristics of false teachers described in this chapter? Describe your experience. How did you respond?

Works, being inanimate things, cannot glorify God,
although they can, if faith is present, be done to
the glory of God.

—Martin Luther

Responsible for What We Produce

Paul has been arguing almost nonstop in favor of the true gospel—salvation based on the finished work of Christ, not our own works. Now he paints a picture that compares what these two "modes of existence" look like in real life. He will show that these two viewpoints have consequences for everyday living. The bottom line is, the way we view our salvation has profound implications for the way we live our Christian life.

What Paul is going to show in this section is that those who are free in Christ and empowered by the Holy Spirit will serve one another in love and will produce spiritual fruit. By contrast, those who are slaves to the law and empowered by the flesh will fight with one another and produce works of the flesh. It's a matter of different products from different sources.

And it's not like we don't have a choice in the matter. Just as we have a responsibility to stay free by not getting "tied up again in slavery to the law" (5:1), we have a responsibility to produce spiritual fruit by letting "the Holy Spirit guide" our lives (5:16).

Chapter 12

New Life in the Spirit

Galatians 5:13-26

What's Ahead

- Free to Serve One Another in Love (5:13-15)
- Free to Live According to the Holy Spirit (5:16-18)
- What the Flesh Produces (5:19-21)
- What the Holy Spirit Produces (5:22-26)

As we approach this section, it's important to realize again that Paul is not addressing people whose eternal destiny hangs in the balance. As Scot McKnight points out, this is not about the Galatians being at a fork in the road, with one path leading to heaven and another one leading to hell. The way Paul will explain it, Spirit and flesh are "modes of existence." As a Christian, you have a choice every day—indeed, every moment of your day—between two ways of living: under the control of the Holy Spirit, or under the control of your own passions and desires.

Free to Serve One Another in Love (5:13-15)

As Christians, we are free, but there are two types of freedom: freedom to *serve* and freedom to *sin*. Paul makes it clear that we are to use our freedom to serve. In fact, of the two modes of existence, this is the only one that is truly free, because choosing to sin leads to slavery to the law and to sin.

The Judaizers were trying to make the case that life apart from the law always leads to sin. Paul counters this by saying Christ has delivered us from sin's mastery and has called us to serve one another in love. As Paul will show, this mode of existence is made possible by the inner working of the Holy Spirit as we let Him control us. This is the only way we are truly free.

The ironic thing is that when we live in this Spirit mode, we *aren't* living apart from the law. We are in fact fulfilling the law, which is summarized in this one command: "Love your neighbor as yourself" (5:14). If we choose to live in the other mode—the flesh mode—then instead of loving others we are "always biting and devouring one another" (5:15).

The Real Meaning of Flesh

The word *flesh,* which appears in 5:13, 16, 17, 19, and 24, is translated "sinful nature" in most Bible versions. According to New Testament scholar Walt Russell, a better translation is "body" or "bodily weakness." The body itself is not evil, although it is frail, weak, and limited—and therefore vulnerable to the mastery of sin. The Judaizers wrongly believed that by focusing on the body through such rituals as circumcision and a restricted diet, they could master the body and therefore fulfill the law. The problem is, because our body (or flesh) is vulnerable to sin, anything we do in the flesh is unacceptable to God because our inclination is to satisfy our own passions and desires.

When we accept Christ and His work on the cross, we essentially nail "the passions and desires" of our flesh to His cross and crucify them there (5:24). As A.W. Tozer writes,

> To save us completely Christ must reverse the bent of our
> nature; He must plant a new principle within us so that our
> subsequent conduct will spring out of a desire to promote
> the honor of God and the good of our fellow men.
>
> It's that *desire* that Paul is talking about. The flesh is neutral, but
> it desires what is evil. That's why we need to live under the con-
> trol of the Holy Spirit, who produces in us a desire to do what
> is good.

Free to Live According to the Holy Spirit (5:16-18)

You've seen the cartoon showing some poor critter with a "devil" on one shoulder and an "angel" on the other. There is some moral decision to be made, and the little devil is trying to persuade the critter to do the wrong thing, while the little angel is doing his best to talk the critter into doing the right thing. The point of this fantasy is that we are in a neutral place, with our "good" and "evil" natures warring within us, trying to win us over to the "dark" or the "light" side.

While this makes for a clever cartoon, it's not very good theology. Again, the flesh is not *inherently* sinful, but it is *instrumentally* sinful. In other words, the flesh (or body) is not in itself sinful, but it is a vehicle for sin. The Judaizers thought the law could shift human desire, but the law was never designed to help people overcome their sinful desires. Only Christ working in us through the Holy Spirit can produce the desire to love God and serve one another.

A life of freedom in Christ is living according to the guidance of the Holy Spirit (see 5:16). On a practical level, how does this happen? Well, it doesn't happen by our will or self-discipline. It happens by surrendering our will and letting the Holy Spirit have control of our lives, and it starts with the things we think about. In his letter to the Romans, Paul describes it this way:

> *Those who are dominated by the sinful nature think about sinful things, but those who are controlled by the Holy Spirit think about things that please the Spirit* (Romans 8:5).

In fact, we are commanded to let the Holy Spirit fill us (Ephesians 5:18) because this is the key to living the Christian life. Not only is the Holy Spirit the source of our new life in Christ, but He is also the power to keep it going.

What the Flesh Produces (5:19-21)

Even though the Holy Spirit is in us, it is our responsibility to surrender our will to Him so He can direct our desires, enabling us to produce the thoughts and actions that please and glorify God. Without God's strength and enablement to help us in our weakness and frailty, we are at the mercy of the desires that come from the flesh.

Another way to say it is this: If we don't follow the leading of the Spirit, we *will* follow the leading of the flesh, with the result that we will gratify the desires of the flesh. When we are in this mode, we haven't somehow "lost" our salvation. We are not outside of God's eternal love and care. But when we are living a "fleshly lifestyle" rather than a "spiritual lifestyle," we are outside of God's will, and we are apart from God's guiding influence through the Holy Spirit.

The list Paul gives in 5:19-21 isn't meant to be comprehensive (so if you don't find a particular sin in these verses, it doesn't mean it's got the Holy Spirit Seal of Approval). But the list isn't abstract either. It's more of a sampler of the kinds of sins everyone knows. Some have said that these sins fall into certain categories, such as sexual, religious, social, and drinking sins. But the descriptions seem to have no particular pattern or order, which is a lot like sin itself. In the next section we're going to see that the qualities that come from a life surrendered to the Holy Spirit do have a certain rhyme and reason. There's a beauty in their order. Not so with these sins that come from the flesh.

We don't have to tell you how chaotic and out of control you feel when your mind and body are not under the control of the Holy Spirit. When you are being guided by the impulses and desires of your flesh, you aren't in control. You think thoughts that would embarrass you if others could hear them. You do things you are later ashamed of.

Worst Ad Campaign Ever

There is an ad campaign for a well-known city in Nevada that says, "What happens in Vegas, stays in Vegas." That has to be the worst advertising slogan ever developed, because it blatantly tells people that satisfying their fleshly desires is perfectly okay—and even encouraged—as long as no one you know and respect (like your family) finds out about it. Wrong! Everything we do to satisfy the flesh has consequences, even if "nobody" sees.

What the Holy Spirit Produces (5:22-26)

Whenever you see a *but* in Scripture, get ready for a contrast. That's what we see in the next series of verses. In contrast to the characteristics produced by someone surrendered to the flesh, Paul lists the characteristics produced by someone surrendered to the Holy Spirit. Notice that these qualities are not *fruits*, but *fruit*. This is the total picture of someone living according to their new life in the Holy Spirit. The nine character qualities are a unified whole, giving us a picture of a true Christian lifestyle. John Stott clusters what he calls "nine Christian graces" into three categories:

- *Love, joy, peace.* These virtues point to our relationship with God. Our first love should be for God, our joy should be in God, and our peace should be first and foremost with God.

- *Patience, kindness, goodness.* These three virtues refer to our relationship with others. *Patience* is the quality of hanging in there with people, even when they irritate or offend us. *Kindness* reflects a pleasant disposition, and *goodness* stems from our words and deeds towards others.

- *Faithfulness, gentleness, self-control.* These three virtues focus on our inner selves. When we keep our commitments, we are *faithful.* When we act with humility and an attitude of service, we are *gentle.* And when we exercise *self-control*, we are doing the opposite of indulging our flesh.

Notice that the fruit listed here is not the fruit of self-effort. It is the fruit of the Spirit. It is not the flesh that brings about this fruit. It is the Spirit of God who produces these qualities in us, but only as we surrender ourselves to Him.

How Do You Live in the Spirit?

Living according to your new life in the Spirit is not a matter of getting more of the Holy Spirit in your life. When you invite Jesus Christ into your life by faith, you receive all of the Holy Spirit you will ever get—because you get *all* of Him. So the question is not,

"How do you get more of the Holy Spirit?" but instead, "How does the Holy Spirit get more of *you?*" The more control we allow Him to have in our lives, the more we will produce spiritual fruit. Allowing the Holy Spirit to control us isn't a "once-for-all" deal. The Holy Spirit is in us once-for-all, but His control over us is day-by-day and moment-by-moment.

Being controlled by the Holy Spirit is what Paul refers to when he says we are to be "filled" with the Holy Spirit (Ephesians 5:18). It's how we live in the Spirit. The benefits to this Spirit-filled lifestyle are amazing. The Bible tells us that when we are filled with the Holy Spirit, He helps us pray (Romans 8:26-27); He helps us love (1 John 4:11-13); He helps us worship (John 4:24); He helps us in our stress (Romans 8:16); He helps us in our decisions (Galatians 5:25); and He helps us understand God's truth (John 14:26; 1 Corinthians 2:11-12).

Yes, we are free in Christ, but we are to use our freedom, not as an excuse to sin, but as an opportunity to love God and love one another. This is the mark of a Christian lifestyle and true Christian community. The community of those whose desire comes from the flesh is characterized by biting and devouring (5:15) as well as competition and envy (5:26). By contrast, the community of those who are following the Holy Spirit's leading in every part of their lives (5:25) is characterized by mutual love and concern.

◼ ◼ ◼

Study the Word

1. What is your response to the concept that as a Christian, you have a choice between two ways of living—under the control of the Holy Spirit or under the

control of your passions and desires? Explain why
you are only truly free when you are serving others
rather than yourself.

2. There is only one way to live in the Spirit mode.
   What is it? (Hint: It isn't through your own efforts.)
   How does this fulfill the law?

3. Why is it incorrect to think of the flesh (or body)
   as *inherently* sinful rather than *instrumentally* sinful?
   What are the implications of viewing the flesh as
   inherently sinful?

4. Describe the difference between a "fleshly lifestyle"
   and a "spiritual lifestyle."

5. Why are we "out of control" when we are under the control of sin? In what ways does human culture—and ours, specifically—glorify and encourage sin?

6. How could you "measure" your progress in each quality of spiritual fruit?
   • Love

   • Joy

   • Peace

   • Patience

   • Kindness

   • Goodness

   • Faithfulness

   • Gentleness

   • Self-control

7. Write out a "game plan" for how the Holy Spirit can gain more control of your life.

Through the Holy Spirit we *come* to know Christ, and by the Holy Spirit's power we *live* and *grow* in Christ, in the service of the King and in the fellowship of His church.

—*Paul Little*

The Mark of a True Christian

There's a perception in our culture today that the church is full of hypocritical, intolerant people whose favorite pastime is judging others. Sadly, this is a fairly accurate perception. No wonder people are leaving the church! Who wants to go to a place where people are "biting and devouring one another"? As he comes to the end of his letter to the Galatians, Paul is concerned about this. We should be concerned as well, because such actions not only chase people away—they also damage our witness for Christ.

Jesus once said that the love we have for one another demonstrates to the world that we are His followers. If you flip that around, it's even more serious. If we don't show love to each other, the world won't know that Jesus is Lord.

Francis Schaeffer called this characteristic of loving and serving one another the "mark" of a true Christian. In this concluding chapter of Galatians, we are going to find out what that mark looks like. Of course, there's a consequence to truly loving one another. People will actually want to come to church, which means that it may not be so easy to find a place to park. Oh, well—that's a small price to pay for following the Holy Spirit's leading in every part of our lives.

Chapter 13

Living to Please the Spirit

Galatians 6:1-18

What's Ahead

- ▓ The Things Spiritual People Do (6:1-10)
- ▓ Paul Summarizes His Message (6:11-18)

As you read and study this final chapter in Galatians, you're going to notice something very interesting. Throughout this letter, Paul never tires of telling his readers that they cannot win God's favor by doing good works. Yet as he brings his letter to a close, he is telling them, "Let's not get tired of doing what is good" (6:9). What gives? Is Paul contradicting himself?

We've touched on this previously, but let's talk about it again. If we are doing good works and performing certain rituals in order to build ourselves up and win God's favor, we are doing them from our flesh, and they will not amount to a hill of beans in God's eyes. But if we are doing good works because we love God and love our neighbor, then we are doing them because the Holy Spirit is controlling us, and the good we do will be used for God's glory. That's the kind of "good" Paul is talking about.

Now let's take a look at some specific examples of the ways in which Christians love one another in the community of grace known as the church. Notice how these contrast with the conflicts found in those communities where legalism is the norm.

The Things Spiritual People Do (6:1-10)

In the first ten verses of chapter 6, Paul lists five specific things a person who is "godly" (NLT) or "spiritual" (NIV) should do. Pure and simple, spiritual people are those who are led by the Spirit. Their actions fall under the general principle of "loving one another," which applies first to Christian brothers and sisters. Following Francis Schaeffer, we could say that these are five "marks" of a Christian.

Spiritual People Help Others Caught in Sin (6:1)

One of the more shameful characteristics of the church is that Christians have a tendency to "shoot their own wounded." That's a graphic way of saying that we do a poor job of helping people who have been "overcome by some sin" to get "back onto the right path." Paul is calling for those who are godly—that is, spiritually mature—to take the lead in this restorative process. He doesn't specify exactly how this is to be done, but he does advise that we should help the offender with gentleness and humility. In another of his letters, Paul asks that the church forgive, comfort, and show love to someone who has caused trouble and hurt the entire church (2 Corinthians 2:7-8).

Jesus provides specific instructions on how we should approach a fellow believer who sins against us (see Matthew 18:15-17). At first we are to go privately to the person. If that doesn't have an effect, we are to take two or three others as witnesses. If the person still refuses to listen, then the matter is to be taken before the church. The goal in all of this is to win back and restore the errant church member. But even in this noble process, there is some danger. Paul warns, "And be careful not to fall into the same temptation yourself."

Spiritual People Share Each Other's Burdens (6:2-3)

Each member of Christ's body has special spiritual gifts for the building up of all the members (see 1 Corinthians 12 and Romans 12 for a list of spiritual gifts). By the same token, each of us should help carry the burdens of those who have troubles and problems. Presumably this includes people who have fallen into sin, but it also refers to those who just have problems. That includes all of us at one time or another, doesn't it? Of course it does. If any of us think we are above helping others, then we probably think we are too good to admit we need help. Get rid of this pride, says Paul, because "you are only fooling yourself."

Spiritual People Don't Compare Themselves to Others (6:4-5)

Our pride can also cause us to compare ourselves to others. This is the "at least I'm not as bad as that guy" syndrome. People used to call someone with this syndrome "holier than thou." Whatever you call it today, there's no place for it among people who are following the Holy Spirit's leading. We need to keep going back to the core message of Galatians: "You are all one in Christ Jesus" (3:28). Since we are all one in Christ, "we all belong to each other" (Romans 12:5). As we share one another's burdens, we need to take responsibility for our own conduct rather than making critical statements about others.

Spiritual People Pay Their Teachers (6:6)

Here's an interesting verse stuck in the middle of this passage. Is Paul miffed because the Galatians haven't paid him for all the teaching he has done? Not at all. Basically what Paul is saying is that students should support their teachers, whether the instruction is private, in a classroom, or in front of a church congregation. Anyone who teaches the Word of God should be paid (also see 1 Timothy 6:17-18). And this isn't just Paul's opinion. When Jesus sent out 70 disciples in pairs to some towns and villages He planned to visit, He told them, "Don't hesitate to accept hospitality, because those who work deserve their pay" (Luke 10:7).

Now, does this mean that if you teach a Bible study, you deserve some sort of compensation? That isn't what Paul is saying. The burden rests with those who are being taught. They are the ones who need to take care of those who teach. Obviously, there are many ways to "pay" teachers. It doesn't necessarily have to be in the form of a paycheck. The "hospitality" Jesus talks about can take many forms. The point is that the student needs to express appreciation for the teacher in a way that is appropriate and fair.

On the other hand, those who teach should evaluate their own motives to make sure they aren't "in it for the money." Perhaps that's why Paul worked as a tentmaker as a way to support himself. Paul isn't suggesting that others follow his example, but it is something some Bible teachers may want to consider.

Sowing and Reaping

Two of the most famous proverbs in the Bible are found in Galatians 6:7-8. The first is best known by its translation in the King James Version of the Bible: "Be not deceived. God is not mocked." The *New Living Translation* says more clearly: "Don't be misled. You cannot mock the justice of God." The other proverb is this: "You will always reap what you sow." Usually these sayings are quoted independently, but when you read them here in

Galatians, one right after the other, you can see that Paul is deliberately linking them together.

Paul draws upon a well-known agricultural metaphor to explain what it means to "sow" and "reap" in a spiritual sense. Not only has God set up the physical world to operate in a cause-and-effect manner, He has also set things up in the moral world to function this way. The writers in the Old Testament knew about this principle. In the book of Job, Eliphaz says to Job, "My experience shows that those who plant trouble and cultivate evil will harvest the same" (Job 4:8). The prophet Hosea writes, "They have planted the wind and will harvest the whirlwind."

Paul takes this sowing and reaping business a step further and applies it to his teaching on flesh and spirit. If we live to satisfy our own fleshly desires, then we will harvest "destruction" (6:8a). But if we live to please the Spirit, we will harvest "eternal" life from the Spirit (6:8b). All of the verses in this section of Galatians have to do with living to please the Spirit, which expresses itself in the ways we love one another. If we are sowing according to the Spirit, then we will do those things that spiritual people do, resulting in a spiritual harvest.

Spiritual People Don't Get Weary in Doing Good (6:9-10)

Anyone who actively engages their spiritual gift or gifts—whether that involves teaching, serving, administrating, giving, or any of the other gifts listed in Scripture—knows that "doing good things for God" can be rewarding. But it can also be exhausting and discouraging at times. That's why Paul wisely offers some encouragement in the form of a metaphor. Just like the farmer works hard to plant seeds, and then waits expectantly but patiently for the harvest, the hard-working Christian patiently waits for the "harvest of blessing" that will surely come from the spiritual seeds he or she has sown.

And just what is the "harvest"? It could be a heart that is encouraged, or a comforted soul, or physical relief. It could be a wayward person brought back to the Lord. The result may not come right away, but it will come, even if the person sowing the seeds of good works doesn't know about it. In fact, we may never know this side of heaven if our good words actually did any good. There isn't even a guarantee that the harvest will come in our lifetime. Paul just says that a harvest of blessing will come "at the appointed time."

Paul Summarizes His Message (6:11-18)

Have you ever received an e-mail with the message in all capital letters? YOU CAN ALMOST HEAR THE SENDER SHOUTING AT YOU! As Paul comes to the end of his letter, that's what he is doing. He personally picks up the pen (until now he has been dictating the letter to an assistant) and writes in LARGE LETTERS for special emphasis. And what is it that Paul wants to emphasize? He wants to make sure the Galatians catch the main themes of the gospel of Jesus Christ. Throughout the letter Paul has successfully argued for three major truths of this gospel:

1. The gospel is from God, not man (Galatians 1 and 2);

2. God has delivered us by means of justification by faith in Jesus, not by works of the law (Galatians 3 and 4); and

3. The deliverance from this present evil age and true freedom from the power of sin are possible only through Christ and the power of the Holy Spirit (Galatians 5 and 6).

Now, to simplify things even more, Paul reduces these three arguments to two themes:

- *Christianity is inward rather than outward.* The Judaizers want to make Christianity a religion based on outward signs and performance. Paul makes it clear that our relationship with Christ is not based on outward things of the flesh, but on an inner work of the Spirit. Galatians 6:15 sums it up:

  It doesn't make any difference now whether we have been circumcised or not; what counts is whether we really have been changed into new and different people (TLB).

- *Christianity is all about Christ, not us.* When we base our relationship with God on our works rather than Christ's work, it becomes all about us. When we build our salvation on the things we do—whether it's circumcision, baptism, speaking in tongues, or any human effort, no matter how noble—Christianity becomes a human, cross-less religion, no different than any of the other human religions out there. But Christianity is not like the other religions. Christianity is all about Christ and His cross, which the world views as "foolish." Paul understands this:

  I know very well how foolish it sounds to those who are lost, when they hear that Jesus died to save them. But we who are saved recognize this message as the very power of God (1 Corinthians 1:18 TLB).

The Galatians are wondering if the finished work of Christ is enough to make them acceptable to God. Here at the end of the letter, Paul lays his cards on the table and lets the "foolish Galatians" know just where he stands:

As for me, God forbid that I should boast about anything except the cross of our Lord Jesus Christ. Because of that cross, my interest in all the attractive things of the world was killed long ago, and the world's interest in me is also long dead (6:14).

This is the attitude we need to have. This world is not our home. As John Stott says, "We and the world have parted company." Before our supernatural encounter with the living Christ, we were desperate for the world's approval. But now that we have been changed into "new and different people," our hope is in the One who saved us, not in the world that calls Him foolish. We are God's new people—Jews and Gentiles alike. Like Paul, we belong to Jesus. There is no higher calling and no greater honor.

■ ■ ■

Study the Word

1. What kind of good works will never win God's favor? What kind of good works come out of a life controlled by the Holy Spirit? Is it possible for these two categories of "works" to look the same? What's the difference?

2. Why does Paul issue this warning to those who help

others caught in sin: "And be careful not to fall into the same temptations yourself."

3. Why is it easier for some of us to help other people with their problems than admit we need help too? What benefit do we gain by sharing our troubles with others?

4. What are some ways to "pay" a Bible teacher other than giving money? Why do you think Paul made such an issue of paying those who teach us?

5. Give some examples of how God has set up the physical world to operate in a cause-and-effect manner. Do the same for the moral world. What do you think Paul means when he writes that those who live to satisfy their fleshly desires will harvest "destruction"?

6. Have you ever gotten weary or discouraged because you were doing good things? What happened? Have you ever resented someone because they didn't recognize something you did for them? Does it help you to know that a harvest of blessing will come at the appointed time? How?

7. Have you truly parted company with the world? If not, what needs to happen in your life?

Dig Deeper

*W*henever we write a book about God and His Word, we do a lot of research and reading. Here are the main books we used to write this study on Galatians. If you want to dig deeper into this amazing letter and the Bible, here's where we would suggest you start.

Commentaries

It's a good idea to have a full Bible commentary in your library. One of the best is *The Bible Knowledge Commentary,* edited by John Walvoord and Roy Zuck, which comes in two volumes. We used the New Testament volume and found it very helpful.

The New Testament volume of Lawrence Richards's *Bible Background Commentary* is useful for bigger-picture cultural and doctrinal issues.

Probably our favorite book-by-book commentary series is the NIV Application Commentary. The volume *Galatians,* by Scot McKnight, is outstanding, both for its deep insights and also for the contemporary applications of the lessons in Galatians.

Max Anders is the editor of an excellent series called the Holman New Testament Commentary. He is also the author of the commentary in that series called *Galatians, Ephesians, Philippians & Colossians*. Wonderful insights given in everyday language.

The Message of Galatians by John R.W. Stott might just be the best book in the bunch. Dr. Stott is both an able Bible scholar and a warmhearted pastor.

G. Walter Hansen's *Galatians*, part of the IVP New Testament Commentary Series, offers some unique perspectives.

Two of the more scholarly commentaries on Galatians are by R. Alan Cole (often cited by other writers) and Walter Russell, whose book, *The Flesh/Spirit Conflict in Galatians*, was very helpful to us.

General Bible Study Helps

It's good to have a solid overview of the Bible, and we have two recommendations. First is a book that is very popular as a college-level textbook: *A Survey of the New Testament* by Robert Gundry. The other book you may want to add to your library is *Knowing the Bible 101* by us (hey, we had to get a plug in somewhere). It's the bestselling book in the Christianity 101 series for a reason: It will help you better understand and appreciate God's amazing Book.

Bible Translations

Obviously you can't study Galatians or the Bible without the primary source—the Bible! People often ask us, "Which Bible translation should I use?" We recommend that your primary study Bible be a *literal* translation (as opposed to a paraphrase), such as the *New International Version* (NIV) of the Bible or the *New American Standard Bible* (NASB). However, it's perfectly acceptable to use a Bible paraphrase, such as *The Living Bible* or *The Message,* in your personal devotional reading.

Our personal choice for Bible study is the *New Living Translation* (NLT), a Bible translation that uses a method called "dynamic equivalence." This means that the scholars who translated the Bible from the original languages (Hebrew and Greek) used a "thought for thought" translation philosophy rather than a "word for word" approach. In the final analysis, the Bible that's best for you is the Bible you enjoy reading because you can understand it.

A Word About Personal Pronouns

When we write, we prefer to capitalize all the personal pronouns that refer to God, Jesus, and the Holy Spirit. These would include *He, Him, His,* and *Himself.* However, not all writers follow this practice, and there's nothing wrong with that. In fact, personal pronouns for God were not capitalized in the original languages, which is why you'll find that many English Bible translations use *he, him, his,* and *himself.*

Download a Deeper Experience

Bruce and Stan are part of a faith-based online community called ConversantLife.com. At this Web site, people engage their faith in entertainment, creative arts, science and technology, global concerns, and other culturally relevant topics. While you're reading this book, or after you have finished reading, go to www.conversantlife.com/101 and use these icons to read and download additional Christianity 101 material from Bruce and Stan:

 Resources: Download study guide materials for personal devotions or a small-group Bible study.

 Videos: Click on this icon for interviews and video clips on various topics.

 Blogs: Read through blogs and articles and comment on them.

 Podcasts: Stream ConversantLife.com podcasts and audio clips.

conversant life .com

engage your faith

Christianity 101® Studies

Now That You're a Christian

If you're a new believer, you'll connect with these honest, encouraging responses to questions that new Christians often have. You'll discover what God has done for humanity, how you can know Him better, and how you can reflect the love of Christ to people around you.

Bible Prophecy 101

In their contemporary, down-to-earth way, Bruce and Stan present the Bible's answers to your end-times questions. You will appreciate their helpful explanations of the rapture, the tribulation, the millennium, Christ's second coming, and other important topics.

Creation & Evolution 101

In their distinctive, easy-to-access style, Bruce Bickel and Stan Jantz explore the essentials of creation and evolution and offer fascinating evidence of God's hand at work. Perfect for individual or group use.

Knowing the Bible 101

Enrich your interaction with Scripture with this user-friendly guide, which shows you the Bible's story line and how each book fits into the whole. Learn about the Bible's themes, terms, and culture, and find out how you can apply the truths of every book of the Bible to your own life.

Knowing God 101

Whatever your background, you will be inspired by these helpful descriptions of God's nature, personality, and activities. You will also find straightforward responses to the essential questions about God.

Bible Answers to Life's Big Questions

Using hundreds of questions from readers, Bruce and Stan tackle some of the biggest issues about life and living the Christian faith, including, *What happens when we die? Is Christ the only way to salvation? How can we know there is a God? Is the Bible true?*

Growing as a Christian 101

In this fresh look at the essentials of the Christian walk, Bruce Bickel and Stan Jantz offer you the encouragement you need to continue making steady progress in your spiritual life.

World Religions and Cults 101

This study features key teachings of each religion, quick-glance belief charts, biographies of leaders, and study questions. You will discover the characteristics of cults and how each religion compares to Christianity.

Christianity 101® Bible Studies

Genesis: Discovering God's Answers to Life's Ultimate Questions

"In the beginning" says it all. Genesis sets the stage for the drama of human history. This guide gives you a good start and makes sure you don't get lost along the way.

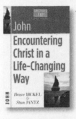

John: Encountering Christ in a Life-Changing Way

This study reveals who Jesus is by demonstrating the dramatic changes He made in the lives of the people He met, including Nicodemus, the woman at the well, Lazarus, and John, "the disciple whom Jesus loved."

Acts: Living in the Power of the Holy Spirit

Bruce and Stan offer a straightforward look at the ongoing ministry of Jesus through the church. They highlight the drama of the early Christians' triumph over darkness and their explosive growth from a band of 120 fearful followers to a thriving, worldwide church.

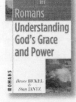

Romans: Understanding God's Grace and Power

Paul's letter to the church in Rome is his clearest explanation and application of the good news. This fresh study of Romans assures you that the Gospel is God's answer to every human need.

1 & 2 Corinthians: Finding Your Unique Place in God's Plan

This enlightening study explores the apostle Paul's helpful responses to issues that churches continue to face today: maintaining unity in the church, exercising spiritual gifts, and identifying authentic Christian ministry.

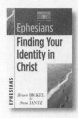

Ephesians: Finding Your Identity in Christ

Verse for verse, the book of Ephesians is one of the most profound, powerful, and practical books in the Bible. This guide reveals the heart of Paul's teaching on who believers are in Christ.

Philippians/Colossians: Experiencing the Joy of Knowing Christ

This new 13-week study of two of Paul's most intimate letters will inspire you to know Christ more intimately and maintain your passion and vision. Filled with helpful background information, up-to-date applications, and penetrating, open-ended questions.

Galatians: Walking in God's Grace

The apostle Paul blows the lid off fake, "rules-added" Christianity and describes life in God's Spirit, through His grace—which is still God's way of freeing you to live out your full potential as His child.

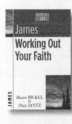

James: Working Out Your Faith

James is bursting with no-nonsense guidance to help you grow in practical ways, including perceiving God's will, maintaining a proper perspective on wealth and poverty, and demonstrating true wisdom in your speech and actions.

Revelation: Unlocking the Mysteries of the End Times

Have you ever read the final chapters of the Scriptures, only to finish with more questions than answers? Bruce and Stan help you understand Revelation's encouraging message and apply it to your life today.